MAU G

Rick Cris.

A Glimpse of Glory

My Journey to Heaven and Back

Rick East

with coauthor Yvonne Erwin

WestBow
PRESS
A DIVISION OF THOMAS NELSON

WestBow Press books may be ordered through booksellers or by contacting:

WestBow Press
A Division of Thomas Nelson
1663 Liberty Drive
Bloomington, IN 47403
www.westbowpress.com
1-(866) 928-1240

ISBN: 978-1-4908-0378-4 (sc)
ISBN: 978-1-4908-0379-1 (hc)
ISBN: 978-1-4908-0377-7 (e)

Library of Congress Control Number: 2013914060

Printed in the United States of America.

WestBow Press rev. date: 08/08/2013

To:

- My heavenly Father
- James (Rusty) Breazeale
- Reverend Larry Brunner

He who overcomes, I will make him a pillar in the temple of My God, and he shall go out no more. I will write on him the name of My God and the name of the city of My God, the New Jerusalem, which comes down out of heaven from My God. And I will write on him my new name.

—Revelation 3:12

CONTENTS

Acknowledgments ix

Prologue xi

1. The Early Years 1
2. A Change of Direction 11
3. Life-Changing Faith 21
4. Rusty 26
5. Larry..31
6. God Repairs Years of Damage..33
7. Toby 40
8. A Nun on the Plane 50
9. Teaching Class 53
10. My Mother's Passing 55
11. Something Evil 61
12. The Illness... 64
13. The Fight Begins 68
14. The Rapid-Response Team..70
15. The City of Light (New Jerusalem, Heaven)...................72
16. A Chorus of Prayer..75

17. Heavenly Bliss and Joy Beyond Imagination 77
18. A Revelation 79
19. You Must Go Back..82
20. You Must Tell Others..85
21. A Complete Absence of Evil...88
22. Live a Life of Righteousness 91
23. Days of Recovery 94
24. Faith's Perspective (written by my wife)...........................96
25. A Scientific Mystery..104
26. What a Victory 107
27. To Those Who Doubt 110
28. An Urgent Mission 112
29. God's Grace 115
30. Obedience... 117
31. Only Trust Him 120
32. Heaven Can Be Yours 123

Epilogue...131
About the Author...137
About the Coauthor 139
Synopsis for A Glimpse of Glory 141

ACKNOWLEDGMENTS

"Thank you" is just not adequate appreciation for those who helped and encouraged this book to be written and the good news of the gospel to be spread.

- Faith East, my loving wife, soul mate, mother to our two children, grandmother to our two grandchildren, and great grandmother to our great grandson.
- Tamara Hunter and husband Mark, and Jason East and wife Jessie, our children.
- Hayley and Trey Hunter, our grandchildren.
- Easton Hunter, our great grandson.
- Keith Day, my cousin who was more like a brother.
- Reverend Hosea Bilyeu, our pastor and source of inspiration.
- The Reverend Edward Armstrong and his wife Carolyn, our small-group leaders.
- All of the members of the Armstrong Faith Family.

- A special thanks to Nick Weyland, who helped and encouraged this book to be written. Thank you so much, Nick.
- Reverend Mike Eklund and his wife Debbie. What a blessing you have been to Faith and me.
- To the health-care professionals at Mercy Hospital. Without their efforts, I would not be writing this book. God gave them the wisdom and skill to save my life.
- Reverend Larry Brunner, who led me to Christ when I needed salvation so desperately.
- The late James (Rusty) Breazeale, who introduced me to my future wife in 1967.

PROLOGUE

G od does the most incredible things with the most unlikely people.

Life is a journey, and we will be judged by the impact we have on those around us.

My pastor, Hosea Bilyeu, once said in a sermon that we should live out loud. Every Christian has a story, and we should tell it. We should tell it with pride and tell it often.

My story began sixty-three years ago and is still in progress. The story I am about to relate to the readers of this book could have ended, and my life would have ended in a most unremarkable way. God chose another outcome. God is no doubt the master storyteller, and the twists and turns shaping my life could have never been predicted by even the best of the best fortune-tellers.

One of my favorite sayings is "Life is what happens while we are making other plans." I do not know who said that, but it is so true.

My life, or I should say, God's life that I live, became quite remarkable on the evening of December 25, 2012, Christmas Day. History records that Christ our Savior was born on December

25. Was it just a coincidence? If it was, it had to be one of many in a long progression of coincidences. From my perspective, it simply could not have been merely a coincidence. There is too much history indicating that what happened to me was God's handiwork.

God is the great Master and Creator. I am just a small piece of his creation, a grain of dust in the midst of His magnificent creation. His majesty and intellect simply can't be reasoned or understood within my humble and simple intellect. It would be like the wooden head of a puppet trying to outthink the puppet master and to anticipate his next move.

I will lay before you the evidence, and you can be the judge. All of the evidence simply would not fit within this book, so I will cover just the most important events.

My life has been crafted by the Master's hand, and I am simply along for the ride. There have been times that I thought God was just messing with me, reminding me just who was really in charge. Then there have been other times when His communication with me really became serious. Either way, I am so happy that God was in control. I could have ruined something that was to turn out really wonderful.

I have read books and heard stories about near-death experiences and recall how they strengthened my faith in God. I had no idea that one day I would have a similar experience.

"Now faith is the substance of things hoped for, the evidence of things not seen" (Heb. 11:1).

I no longer need faith that God is real, that Christ did go to prepare a place for us, and that the Bible is true and the written word of God.

I have been to heaven and experienced its glory; the unseen has become the seen.

I was sent back to tell others of heaven's glory and to warn them of the other option.

"In My Father's house are many mansions; if it were not so, I would have told you. I go to prepare a place for you" (John 14:2).

CHAPTER 1

The Early Years

I was born into and raised in what is today called a dysfunctional family. My first memories are from a time when my mother, father, two sisters, and I were living in an abandoned farmhouse on my grandfather's farm in Webster County, Missouri.

My first memory comes from when I was about five years old. I said my father lived with us; the fact of the matter was he was gone most of the time. He claimed to be out trying to make a living for us by driving a truck. I think he had a lot of distractions; as a result, we had to live as we did.

My mother was a proud person, too proud to ask for more charity than she already received from my grandparents.

It was my grandparents who provided the old farmhouse, the electricity for the lights, and some of our food. Being a farm family in 1955, they too struggled to survive. Money was in short supply. My grandparents traded farm produce like eggs and butter to the MFA Exchange in Conway, Missouri, for things that they needed, such as sugar and flour.

The old house could hardly be considered shelter at all. The roof leaked when it rained, and the wind blew straight through the doors and windows. I remember having to stand near the old woodstove to stay warm. Our beds were piled so high with blankets and bedding that we could barely roll over, we were so weighed down. But all of that was what we had to do to survive the long, cold Missouri nights.

Field mice came and went without being disturbed. It was an ongoing battle between humans and rodents to keep food from being devoured by the tiny pests.

My mother slipped deeper and deeper into her own dark world of depression, a world where reason and hope did not exist; she felt her plight was hopeless. Father lived as if he hadn't a care in the world.

Mother would, years later, confide in me that she deeply regretted getting involved with the first man who had ever given her attention. Now with three young children and a worthless husband who did not care if his family had the basic needs of life, she felt the hopelessness of her situation. There are people who simply do not have the capacity or ability to love or have compassion for another living soul, and my father was one of them.

Father would inadvertently reveal to me the main source of his affection. He took me to a pool hall one evening when he was supposed to be looking after me because I had my right leg in a cast from a recent surgery. It became obvious he was good at the game, very good. He was a pool hustler and a gambler; this was how he spent much of his time and money. He was good, but there were better and he lost a lot. He would only work when he needed money to support his gambling habit. He never came home drunk, and I never heard of him chasing women or carousing around in other ways.

Being stranded away from the city with no way to provide for herself and her children, Mother felt completely without hope for a better future. Finally my mother came to believe she could not endure any more. Father had been gone for several days. The only food we had left was buckwheat pancakes mixed together with water and fried in bacon grease; everyone kept bacon grease to cook with in those days. We were starving one day at a time, living only by the hands of our grandparents, who brought us what they could. Mother saw no hope for her children. She knew that if she were gone, people who could care for them would adopt her children.

One cold night in March, right after my fifth birthday, Mother waited until she heard the rumble of Father's old truck pull up the farm road and stop in front of the house. Father had come home, but it did not matter, Mother put the barrel of a 22-caliber rifle to her chest and pulled the trigger.

My sisters and I were all in one bed, buried under tons of blankets. We never heard the shot; we were not aware of what was going on.

Father drove to our grandparents' house, just a quarter mile away, to get help. When our grandparents arrived, my sisters and I were bundled up and taken to stay with relatives. One of my uncles drove Mother to the hospital in Springfield, Missouri.

We learned later that the bullet missed its mark by a fraction of an inch, and my mother lived. She spent weeks in the hospital recovering physically and even longer recovering from a complete nervous breakdown.

For months I lived with aunts and uncles, I had an older sister approximately two years older than me and a younger sister who was approximately two years younger. We were initially sent to different locations to live. We had eight uncles on my mother's side of the family, so there were plenty of options. We were eventually taken to stay with my grandparents. On the weekends, we would go to visit my mother at the mental hospital in Nevada, Missouri.

Each time we left her, there was so much sadness and crying. I wondered if it was good for her to see us. As part of her recovery, she learned to sew and made two Raggedy Ann dolls for my sisters and a Raggedy Andy doll for me.

She would later make more of those dolls and give one to each of her grandchildren and children from the neighborhood.

Mother returned home after about a year. Since it was such a long time ago, when I was only five, my memories are not clear. Exact details are gone now but it was a traumatic event burned into my memory. My father moved us to Springfield, where he said he could do a better job of providing for us. That didn't happen. In fact, things did not improve until my mother went to work at a restaurant across town, soon after we moved in to our rented house in Springfield. My father went to Joliet Illinois to work in the Caterpillar plant located there. Mother was left to fend for us alone. My father did send a little money home that helped some. Mother finally realized that for things to improve, she would have to take charge and do things for herself. My father did not last long at the job in Ill, so he soon came home and found work here in Springfield.

Mother left us three kids with a neighbor while she worked.

We at least had food and a few clothes. About a year later she y moved us to a four-room house next door to the restaurant where she worked.

She no longer had to ride a city bus for an hour to and from work each day while my father was out hustling pool and whatever else occupied him. My mother's new independence infuriated him, and they fought constantly. He wanted her to quit working, and she knew if she did, we would end up back in that old farmhouse starving again.

By the time I was in the third grade, the fighting had escalated to the point that my father was threatening to kill the whole family by setting fire to the house my mother rented.

I slept on the couch in the living room of the tiny four-room house. My father would sit in one of the chairs with a five-gallon can of gas at his side as he smoked. He would keep the fight going and make just enough noise to keep my mother and me from sleeping. I believe he thought that if he could keep her from sleeping, she could not work the following day and would eventually lose her job.

Thankfully, the good people she worked for were very understanding and sympathetic.

Because Father kept me from sleeping, my schoolwork suffered. I was having difficulty learning to read. My teacher grew more and more frustrated with my lack of progress.

She began to bring me to the front of the class to make me read out loud, pulling my chair up next to hers and telling me to read to the class.

When I stumbled over a word, she became furious and would hit me on top of the thigh with a heavy wooden paddle, and yell, "You know that word; now say it," or, "You're going to learn to read if I have to beat it into you."

During those occasions, I couldn't even see the words on the paper through my tears. My classmates sat in stupefied horror watching, and some even cried as I did.

I became the outcast of the class. I suppose my classmates were either afraid my predicament would rub off on them or they just didn't want to have anything to do with such a dummy.

I promised myself that when I was older and big enough, I would look this teacher up and let her experience the pain and humiliation she inflicted on me.

As a further insult, I was held back a year as a result of my slow learning. I suppose the daily beatings in front of the class were not enough embarrassment and humiliation.

When I was in the fifth grade, my mother took me to a children's free clinic for my feet, because they hurt all the time. The doctors told her I needed an operation on both feet to correct a deformed bone that caused me to have extremely flat feet.

I remember the first operation. I was prepped and readied for surgery by a nurse, then left in the room alone. When the nurse came to take me to the operating room, I was still alone and crying.

My mother told me that if my father came home, she would get him to bring her to the hospital before the surgery so that we could see each other beforehand.

I realized what had happened, Mother never learned to drive a car and either had to rely on my father to drive her or ride a bus. The bus did not run early enough to get her to the hospital before the surgery. The crippled children's clinic arranged for surgeries to be performed by surgeons who donated their time. The free surgeries would be performed very early, before the surgeons' usual schedule.

The right foot was operated on first, and then the left a year later. For two years, just being able to walk was a delicious luxury to me. My classmates, and even I now, thought that I was mentally deficient and physically defective.

Back in those days, there was no Americans with Disabilities Act that dictated there had to be an elevator or a handicapped ramp or any such device providing for the safety of someone on crutches. Several times a day, I would climb to the third floor at

Tefft Elementary School and then back down. The stairs were narrow, steep, and high, with very low handrails. I was terrified; my classmates would become impatient and scamper past while I fought to maintain my balance. Only one reason could explain why I did not fall to my death on those steps; it was the grace of God and His protection.

I had to learn how to walk and then run at a time when other boys my age were playing Little League baseball and other sports. I could only look on from the sidelines, once again set apart and excluded.

My feet eventually healed. I was big; I was a strong person, sought after by high school coaches to give sports a try. While I appreciated the attention, the damage was done. The skills and knowledge that my peers had been developing for years were all new to me, and I could not make up the deficit. As a result, those who were the first people to show me any attention were rewarded with disappointment, and I with failure.

I turned to other interests. I enjoyed working on cars and driving them. This was something I could do that others my age knew little about. I was a junior in high school when my mother finally left my father after years of abuse and making every effort to make her marriage work. My mother, my younger sister, and I were living in a one-bedroom apartment; my older sister was already married and left the household. I was attending a new school, trying to make new friends and start a new life.

November 1958 at my grandparents' farm near Conway, Missouri
and my cousins with whom I enjoyed spending time.

Back row from left to right, Keith Day, Rick East (bending over)
Andrea East, Linda Day, and Carolyn Day, being held by Nancy East.

Front row from left to right, R.C. Day, Debby Day,
Martha Day, Diane Day and Donna Day.

May 21, 1951 at my grandparents' farm near Conway, Missouri.
My mother, shown here with her immediate family.

All last names are Day except for my mother
whose last name was East at that time.

Back row from left to right my grandmother Mable
Day, Edward, O.G., my mother Mary Kathryn, Joe
Bill, my grandfather Orville Day and Johnnie.

Front row from left to right Jack, Don, Raymond and Rolive.

My mother, Mary Kathryn Day-East.

CHAPTER 2

A Change of Direction

I was seventeen in 1967. I owned a car I bought with down payment money I had worked for and saved up, I also had a trade-in that I bought the same way. I still had to make payments on a small loan to cover the balance of the cost. The car was a beautiful 1964

Chevrolet Impala Super Sport in desert beige, with a convertible top. What a cool car—a four speed on the floor, positrack rear end, and a 300-horsepower 327 C.I. engine. It was my pride and joy, and I drove it with great skill and dexterity. I knew the car mechanically from bumper to bumper. When driving that beautiful machine, I and the car were one; it was my first love affair. The car responded to me as though it knew how much I adored it. I worked on it constantly as often as I had time and money, improving the power and handling.

One cold, rainy winter Saturday, I was out driving around when an old Buick with faded paint approached the intersection directly in front of me. For a moment it looked as if the car was going to stop, as it should have, at the stop sign. But it sped up and was suddenly in front of me. Anticipating that the driver might run the stop sign, I covered the brake with my foot, but it was not enough; I should have slowed or stopped altogether. My screaming intuition was correct, but it was too late.

The hood of my beloved Chevy buckled at the impact, with the heavy old Buick hitting just behind the driver's door. I watched as the Buick's driver's side door swung open as the car spun around. An elderly lady flew out and rolled wildly across the pavement. It was as if I were watching a movie; time slowed down, and everything was happening in jerky, slow motion.

In the clear and certain terror of that moment, I realized I was in a much more serious situation than a mere fender bender. Total, naked awareness was setting in. One life had just come to its end, and I knew that there were others whose lives would change because of one moment in time, this moment.

How I did it, I don't know, but I jumped from my crumpled car and ran to the lady, lying bloodied and twisted at the edge of the intersection. When I reached her, she was not breathing as blood ran from her open eyes, nose, and mouth. Her upper torso was twisted from her lower body in an unnatural way. Standing there, I felt that my life had just ended as well. It was apparent that she was beyond help.

The police came and took my statement and the statements of other witnesses, all routine matters. The witnesses told the police there was nothing I could have done to prevent the accident; the lady simply ran through the stop sign without warning.

As the afternoon light began to dim and the gentle rain became a downpour, an ambulance arrived. EMTs loaded the body of the lady, and then slowly drove away with only their running lights, no doubt going directly to the morgue.

Two wreckers came, hooked up to my car and the old Buick, and hauled them away as I watched them disappear into the distance. The police officers got back into their cars and drove off. I was left standing alone on the corner in the cold rain. My light jacket was not enough to keep the cold and wet away from my skin. Pelting rain plastered my hair across my face, and the rain washed away my tears, which were now flowing in great torrents.

I was only seventeen, but life had already been filled with such tremendous torment—what more would I have to endure? Rain and cold only added another layer of insult and injury. In so much misery, I barely noticed Mother Nature's disrespect. I truly believe that it is impossible for a person to die of a broken heart. If it was possible, I would have died at that moment.

In a very few minutes, my world was the coldest kind of surreal. I watched the rain wash the pool of the unknown lady's blood into the gutter, spinning away until it was out of sight, diluted in leaves and other debris spinning along the same way. So then the mess was cleaned up, the blood washed away, and in no time, traffic and life for the rest of the world resumed normalcy.

My clothes were soaked through; I stood in that spot that long. Finally I started to walk and eventually reached one of the busiest streets in town.

All of my life, I harbored a dream, a dream buried deep but still alive and real for me. Oh how I longed for a normal life with two loving parents, a mother and a father who would both care for me, love me, teach me things I needed to know about life, and provide for me. In my mind I could see a beautiful little home with window boxes and a garden growing in the summer sun behind a white picket fence. A home where my mother was waiting for me to return from school with cookies and milk in hand and a tender kiss for my forehead. A home where my father would return from work at the end of the day and play catch with me after dinner.

My heart was so broken, I felt desolate. The enormity of the reality of my life versus what I wished my life entailed was crushing. The fact that my dream was just an impossible fantasy was a kick to the gut that sent me reeling; it was another vicious and unavoidable torment. I would never forget the vision of the sweet, unknown, little lady, who looked like my grandmother, careening across the blacktop. The sight would never leave my memory. What hope was left for me? I couldn't see any strand of hope to grab onto; I was lost indeed. No hope. No hope left that the normal life I had once dreamed of could ever happen.

I formulated a plan as I walked. I, like my mother before me, would attempt to end my miserable life. I would stand on the median near the intersection and wait for a large truck speeding by, and then step in front at the last moment. Standing on the median, I saw my opportunity and reacted. But something strange happened at the moment I should have died, I was pulled back, as if my center of gravity suddenly shifted behind me.

I then heard a voice that said, "Hell is much worse than this." The voice came with a strange reassurance that somehow things were going to get better.

I had to heed the message, and I began to cry out to God, "What do you want from me? I don't know what to do! Please help me, please help me, God." I didn't know how to pray. I didn't know how to reach out to an unseen, unknown God, a being that I didn't really know I could trust. My cry for help to a God that I really didn't know was all I knew to do.

Somehow from somewhere came that sense of peace and reassurance again. Now with a new sense of hope, I began walking in the direction of the apartment where my mother, sister, and I lived.

The next morning, I knew I had to face the world and return to school and to work. The cold stares from my classmates and the accompanying ugly whispers cut me to the bone as I walked past them. I never felt so alone in my life.

And yet, I understood the death of the old lady wasn't my fault. It could have happened to any other driver, anyone driving on that street on that day at that time. She drove through the intersection. What happened was horrible, but it wasn't my fault. One of the lady's relatives called and talked with my mother and was very kind in that regard. They assured Mother there was nothing I could have done. They told her that just a second or two different, and I could have been the one making the trip to the morgue.

A family was leaving the home on the corner and witnessed the crash. They told the police the lady driving the old Buick caused the accident. But why did this happen to someone in such a fragile mental state as I? Why would I have to relive the terrifying vision each time memories were recalled?

Facing my peers was equally terrifying; I knew what they were thinking. *He must have done something wrong. He must have been speeding or just was not looking.* Even though none of these ideas were true, their stares burned gaping holes in my emotional state.

My stomach was one big knot, and my fingers hurt from gripping the steering wheel so hard when I had braced for the impact. Both knees were deeply bruised from hitting the dash of my beautiful sixty-four. From class to class I walked, trying to hold my head up and ignore those who just did not understand. Still dazed, I completed the day without much outward emotion, but

God knew I was completely breaking up on the inside. Desperate, my desire was to skip work after school that evening. Even though my car was at a body shop across town being repaired, I still had car and insurance payments, so I went on.

Walking the four blocks from Parkview High School to the McDonalds restaurant at 501 West Sunshine, where I worked, I set my resolve to get through the evening shift much the same as I did school that day.

The rain hung around from the day before until a cold front moved in and it began to snow.

The snowstorm continued throughout the evening shift. Customers were scarce that evening, and I tried to let my mind go to a place where the weather was sunny and warm and I felt loved. My grandparents' farm was a place of retreat, where love and comfort were always evident and in abundance, and I longed to go there!

As a consolation, I attempted to bury myself in work to get a grip on what had happened. My way of dealing with this tragic event was to put the whole incident in a box and tuck it away in some hidden corner of my mind. There it would be manageable and convenient. Pain would be dealt with only when needed. My normal life could resume as quickly as the memories faded. That was it: I now had a plan to get back to concentrating on school and my job and put all of this unpleasant mess behind me. It was a new beginning, a regrouping and a reorganization that would not be.

That first night back at work, my long-lost father walked into the lobby, and with all of my coworkers looking on he said, "I heard you killed an old lady." I walked away furious and embarrassed; however, that mean-spirited comment really did me a world of good. It really made me angry, and I began to come out of the depression I was under. The light bulb moment about it was when

I realized that you can't let other people control your life by their feelings toward you.

On my last break of the night, Larry Brunner, the night-shift manager, came back to talk to me and tried to console me.

Larry was a student at Baptist Bible College and was very popular with all of the young men who worked on his shift.

Larry had great compassion for the young men who worked for him. All of us trusted him. We put a lot of stock in what Larry said, what Larry did, and how Larry behaved. Larry himself was a professional at work and humble; he could defuse a situation between employees or between customer and employee easily and with no fallout. He realized that none of us worked for the luxury of having some extra spending money. We all worked after school because we helped not only ourselves but our families as well.

Each night, just before closing time, Larry would say, "Grill, put on twenty-four." Larry knew that most of those burgers would be left over, and he would send the food home with the crew to be eaten by their families. Quite honestly, the burgers were meals for needy family members, meals they might not have had otherwise.

Now on that night, Larry, knowing my car was badly damaged in the accident, offered me a ride home.

It was snowing thick and hard when it was time to leave, and the snow was stacking up fast. I settled into the passenger seat while Larry warmed up the old 1941 Chevy truck he drove. We sat in the drive for a few minutes as the engine warmed, and Larry told me about Jesus and how only Jesus could change my life. I listened, partly because I was anticipating a ride home and partly because what this guy was saying spoke to me. It spoke to me in my heart and my soul. He was speaking to me on a different level than I'd ever heard before.

Larry explained the Roman Road to me, and once I understood what he was saying to me, I accepted Christ as my savior. In that moment, I felt warmth surround me, I felt a warm glow within me, and the glow began to radiate outward, out of my body, expanding and engulfing me, becoming more and more white and pure with every beat of my heart. I knew without a doubt, God had reached down and touched me, filling me with His Holy Spirit.

Sitting in the passenger side of that pickup, I really felt stripped bare; all of the old had been taken away, and I was now clean, new, and forgiven. My complacence was replaced with a new awareness that God is and was and shall ever be the most important part of who I am.

I realized in that moment, God was aware of my agony, and He heard my cries. He was communicating with me on a basic level, on a level I would understand and accept.

Thinking back, the first time was on that street corner, when he held me back and said, "Hell is worse than this." The second time God spoke to me just happened when I accepted salvation. He simply gave me the knowledge of what had happened to me in that moment.

I could not deny that God had reached down and touched me and filled me with His Holy Spirit.

Something truly amazing had just happened. I was full of questions. What now? How does this change things, and what does being a Christian mean? In spite of the questions, I knew that a sudden change had just taken place. A new peace, sense of freedom, and knowing that I had just been forgiven was beginning to spring forth from within me like a flower garden in the warm spring sun.

That night, Larry dropped me at the apartment, and said, "It is your faith that has set you free, and you have a new life now." I was so young then and did not understand exactly what he meant, but accepted the comment and went on my way.

Larry's comment slipped to the back of my mind, and I didn't think anything more of that simple statement until all of the pieces to my life puzzle began coming together some forty-five years later and I went to heaven and come back with this story.

My life was like a pile of puzzle pieces, and only now am I able to step back and see how the pieces all fit together, and it is a beautiful picture. It is one that only the Great Master could create.

In time, I also came to realize that the day the accident ended the life of the sweet little lady, God had called her home.

When my mother spoke to her relatives, they told her that she had been an active Christian for many years and was ready when called.

The Holy Spirit showed me what I was telling people was wrong: I wasn't in the wrong place at the wrong time. God was calling both the lady home and me; she left immediately, while I still had a lot of living for our heavenly Father to take care of. This incident was God preparing my heart and getting me ready to hear and accept his plan of salvation.

Satan wanted me dead. He wanted my soul and my spirit and to drag me down to hell, where I would burn for all eternity. Satan wanted to silence my voice so I could never tell the good news about salvation and the forgiveness of Jesus Christ to other lost people like I had been told.

**My niece Laurie, behind the wheel of my 1964 Impala
SS Convertible in 1967, I loved that car.**

CHAPTER 3

Life-Changing Faith

One simple act of faith created a bond between the Holy Spirit and me that will last for all eternity. The Holy Spirit has communicated with me many times throughout the years and has been my constant guide and companion.

My junior year in high school, I became friends with a student named James Breazeale, nicknamed Rusty, no doubt because of his red hair.

Rusty was a car nut like me and always wanted to drive my car. My Chevy, completely repaired from the accident with the old Buick, drove better than ever, but I would not let Rusty get behind the wheel until I was certain that he could handle that much power. Rusty was just a bit too brave for my liking and a bit too crazy. I was even more protective than ever of my beautiful Chevy convertible.

In the meantime, Rusty kept telling me that I needed to meet his adopted niece. He was certain that we would make a great couple.

Larry, the night-shift manager, told me about a 1958 MG he drove by every day to and from work. It was for sale, and the owner only wanted $350.00 for it. One day I stopped by the gas station where the car was parked and made a deal with the station owner to buy the car for $250.00 and use his station along with his metric tools to reassemble the engine and install it back in the car. He threw in the use of his facilities and tools to get me to buy the car in the condition that it was in, disassembled and in pieces. I suspected he needed the money pretty bad since he reduced his asking price by $100.00. Even with the car's poor condition, I knew it was a great bargain.

Once I got to work on the MG, I discovered it came from Arkansas and had been used for road racing. The engine was out of the car and in pieces inside a big wooden box sitting in a corner of the garage.

The station owner bought the car in that condition, and it had come with all of the correct new parts to completely repair the engine. All I had to do was figure out how to put it back together again correctly.

One sunny spring day, I was working on my new acquisition when Rusty, his sister, and his niece pulled up in the gas station drive. The gas station owner was gone, and I was supposed to wait on customers while he was out. This had become quite a habit for him when I was there. I thought at the time that he was a very trusting person—or an extremely good judge of character.

Rusty introduced me to his niece and his sister, but the niece just sat there, obviously not impressed. I didn't know if it was the ratty work clothes I had on or the oil and grease I was covered in that had made the impression.

She was quite a looker, with blonde hair and big green eyes. I immediately thought, *She is out of my league, and she knows it.*

We talked for a few minutes about the car I was working on, and then Rusty said, "Let's get out and look at it; I want to see it." We walked around the car as I pointed out all of the special equipment it came with. Even though Rusty's niece clearly was not impressed with me, I could not resist checking her out. She had more curves than my 1958 MG. I was impressed. Rusty kept jabbering about my 1964 Chevy and hinting about how badly he wanted to take it for a spin. I knew what he wanted to spin. He wanted to burn rubber and spin the tires.

The tour over, I watched them drive away after I gassed up Rusty's Corvair. I thought, *That's the end of that; I am clearly not her type.*

Monday, the next day at school, Rusty said, "I have my niece's phone number, and she really wants you to call her. She could not stop talking about you all day Saturday."

I said, "You have got to be kidding. Are you just setting me up? She hated me."

"No, no, no, she just didn't want to seem too eager; just call her tonight," Rusty said.

Faith Jones was her name, and when I called her, I said, "Hello, this is Rick East."

She said, "Rick who?" and I thought, *That darn Rusty has set me up again.* Rusty, the constant joker, was always playing tricks. However, joke or not, I did not let it stop me from my intention of asking her out. When I did, she was more eager as she accepted my offer.

Back at the gas station, I had noticed Faith was a very good-looking girl, but after spending some time with her on our first date, I realized she was really gorgeous, with a heart to match. She possessed a rare quality—outward beauty as well as inward beauty.

I could say it was a coincidence, but it was beyond coincidence. Faith and I met just a few weeks after my salvation experience.

But what told me this meeting was beyond mere coincidence was that her name was Faith. The phrase that Larry left me with at the apartment kept playing in my mind: "Your faith has set you free."

After our first date, I knew Faith was the woman I would marry. The Holy Spirit had spoken again, not in an audible voice, but with a simple giving of information, a knowing that something was to be, something of God. I did not share this information with Faith because I was still just learning to trust my newfound source of information.

As the days and weeks passed by, we got to know each other better. I found myself astonished that such a beautiful young girl could fall in love with me, but fall she did.

Like the events in chapter two, I did not fathom the significance, the enormity, until just recently.

I look back now and can only say, "Are you kidding me? Just how blind can a person be?" How could I not understand how important Faith would be to me, both my wife Faith and my spiritual faith?

We now have two grown children, Tamara and Jason, and they have blessed us with two grandchildren and one great grandson. Faith and I have been happily married since August 8, 1969.

Those long-ago feelings of being unloved and totally alone are only ghosts or shadows of a terrible past now. Some believe in love at first sight, and some do not. When Faith and I met, I knew that I would love her forever, and I knew that God made a place for her in my heart and life. I also knew that to keep looking for someone else would be a big mistake. God chose her for me, and who could do a better job of choosing a mate than God? God knows every person's heart. Faith's heart for God and devotion and dedication to her family is unmatched. She adores all of our children and has been a dedicated wife for all of these years. Our heavenly Father certainly knows best.

Faith in 1969 just before we were married.

Rick in 1969.

CHAPTER 4

———⟫•◦•⟪———

Rusty

This chapter is dedicated to James (Rusty) Breazeale. Rusty and his sister, Suzie, called Faith's grandmother Nana. Nana was their babysitter, and they started calling her Nana when they were toddlers. Nana was her name, and no one really remembered her given name.

One evening when their mother came to pick them up, she made a bizarre request. She wanted to know if Nana could just keep the children and care for them. Fearing she could no longer care for them, she told Nana she intended to put them up for adoption. "They think of you as their mother anyway, Nana," she pleaded. "Nana, please? I can't care for the babies anymore. Please do this for me, Nana, please. You don't want them going to the state, and neither do I. You know the stories of what happens to children who do go to the state. Nana, I beg you; take my children."

Nana relented. Seeing the children go off to some unnamed state agency or a foster home was out of the question. Nana and her husband took the children into their home and later adopted them. Their home was warm and cozy, with a vegetable garden in the back and a white picket fence around the front. Nana cooked good meals and washed clothes and made the house feel like home for Rusty and Suzie. The children thrived under her care.

The funny thing was Rusty and Suzie's mother was never heard from again. The speculation in town was that she ran off with a married minister. Some said she drank herself to death in a seedy hotel room in some other town. Still others said that she left town in a big hurry and told the conductor of the train she got on that she was leaving for good, for California and whatever California held for her. No one really ever knew what happened to her. All of that was simply speculation. The point was she never came back to visit her children. No letters came from sunny California, and there were no phone calls. There were no birthday cards, no well wishes at high school graduation, and no Christmas cards.

Rusty and Suzie continued to thrive in Nana's care as much as they could having been abandoned by their parents, as their father was also missing from their lives and we have no knowledge of who he was or what happened to him.

In spite of the harsh reality of their lives, they were happy, well-adjusted children.

My mother finally left my father when I was a junior in high school. That was when I met Rusty. Both of us attended Parkview High. I was beginning to make friends. Rusty and I did not have any classes together, but we met on the bus that carried us to the vocational-technical school after lunch and then back at the end of the day.

We became good friends. Rusty was fun. He had a good nature, and I liked to be around someone who could joke around.

Rusty always found something to laugh about and was one of those people who carried a smile well. It was as if a smile belonged on his face all the time.

After he introduced me to Faith, Rusty met a beautiful young lady, and they were later married. Faith and I remember the joy he found when they were married. Some months later, Rusty announced they were going to start a family. His wife was pregnant! Their son was born just before Rusty received terrible news. He had leukemia. The prognosis was not good. The cancer was at a late stage and progressing fast.

Life moved in fast-forward after the news of Rusty's terminal illness. A few months after the devastating diagnosis, Rusty passed away without seeing his son's first birthday. Although the disease was at a late stage when it was caught, Rusty fought, trying to beat it, to be set free from it. Unfortunately, medical treatment was not as good then as it is today. Rusty's options were severely limited, and he passed, not knowing where he was or who was with him.

Faith and I stood at his bedside as he suffered a seizure, a seizure ending his ability to communicate. His physical body died days later. Rusty was twenty years old on the day of his death. At the time, I took comfort in knowing he loved Jesus and he was a Christian. Rusty always had his new family in church on Sunday. My heart and spirit tell me that Rusty and I will meet again. We will meet again far beyond this world, in fact, in the world I drifted to when I passed from this life to another life. I know, when my final calling comes, Rusty will already be in that place when I arrive. He will be there to welcome me and show me all the glories that heaven has to offer.

Death changes circumstances in a lot of cases. In Rusty's case, his wife took their little boy and moved to Illinois, and we didn't see them again until they came back for a visit with relatives. Faith and I were invited to the family reunion. How pretty it all was! And how poignant: Rusty's son resembled him so much. It broke my heart to look on his face and think of his dead father, my friend, the now saint in heaven. I would gaze at him and wonder if the fun-loving good nature of his father was imbedded in him, and I used to think I hoped so because the boy would need that good nature to cope with life.

More tragedy followed. Rusty's sister, Suzie, passed away some years later, with cancer of the esophagus. Losing Suzie proved to be an acute loss as she left behind a husband, a son, and a daughter, all who loved her beyond measure.

Each Memorial Day since Rusty's death, Faith and I visit his grave and leave flowers on the headstone. So far as we know, there are no living relatives left in the area, and we couldn't, we wouldn't let his memorial go unnoticed. One year, however, we arrived at the cemetery to find flowers left at the gravesite. It was so unexpected. Faith and I have speculated and wondered since who could have left those flowers there and why only that one time.

If it hadn't been for Rusty, Faith and I would never have met; therefore, we made a pledge upon his burial that we would mark the date of his death and burial, and we would visit his gravesite and decorate his stone until the day both of us passed from this earth to the new life in heaven. Since Rusty died, we've not missed a year. It may be me, hobbling along on a cane or a walker, or it may be Faith doing the same one day, but we or one of us will make sure Rusty is remembered until we are in heaven rejoicing with the saints, with him.

James (Rusty) Breazeale   Suzie Breazeale, Rusty's sister

April 1953, just after Faith's grandparents adopted Rusty and Suzie.

Back row from left to right Earl Breazeale, (Nana) Blanche Breazeale, Jewell Jones, (Faith's mother) and Faith in her arms.

Front row Suzie and Rusty.

CHAPTER 5

Larry

This chapter is dedicated to Larry Brunner.

Larry Brunner worked as the night-shift manager at the McDonald's Restaurant at 501 West Sunshine, where I worked as a high school kid. Larry was a fun-loving guy and, like Rusty and me, was a car guy.

Larry was from the Deep South and had a pronounced Georgia accent. Larry brought his family to Springfield because he enrolled in Baptist Bible College. Larry felt the call to the ministry and wanted to be trained in Springfield.

He wasn't a big preacher, but he tended to be available to the young men in his charge as a counselor and friend, more like a big brother than a boss. His inherent wisdom and understanding seemed deeper to me than most big brother figures I'd encountered. Larry was a selfless person, a person who loved others more than himself. That love was demonstrated quite often on the night shift when someone was having problems at home or at school. Larry had a sixth sense about people around him needing help, and before long, that person would be found talking to Larry, even praying with him.

Rusty helped me get a job working with him at the local Ramey's Super Market as a carryout and stocker. I left the McDonald's job to go work there. The Ramey's job paid a lot more money, and it was just three blocks from Faith's house. Faith came in the store sometimes, and the other carryout boys complained seeing me follow her to her car carrying a loaf of bread, a bottle of milk, or some other non-important item she'd purchased just to see me, but I did not care. Just seeing her for five minutes a couple times a week was worth the world to me. Most times, I'd sneak a kiss before she put the car in drive and drove out of sight. If I walked back in the store with a goofy grin on my face, what was it to them?

Faith and I received an invitation to Larry's graduation from BBC. I think that was the last time we saw each other, as God's plan for our lives took us in different directions. Larry and I lost contact when I took the Ramey's job, and he graduated from college and moved away.

I once heard that he moved back to Georgia or Mississippi, where his family ties were. I contacted the Alumni Office at BBC in an attempt to get his contact information, but because of privacy laws, they could not provide me with any information on him. And so, I lost the thread with Larry. I never saw or heard from him again, but I know we will meet again some day when God's timing is right.

CHAPTER 6

God Repairs Years of Damage

Years of struggle in school, believing I was inadequate and slow to learn, left me feeling that I wasn't good for much. The importance of sports was no longer an issue, and my feet were no longer a problem. Lingering doubts about my abilities and questions left unanswered brought me to an awareness of things that happened in school but were never explained. My suspicions were rising regarding my intellectual deficiencies. Learning whatever subject I attempted to learn about seemed to be of no great difficulty. I soon learned that I could conquer any task I set out to achieve, and as a result, I set out to do some research of my own.

An unexpected meeting brought my questions and doubts to the surface. One day, I ran into my old fourth-grade teacher at a restaurant, and I made a joke of being the grade-school idiot. Her reply was immediate and caught me off guard. "You are certainly no idiot; your test scores were always quite high."

I was dumbfounded. My test scores were high? But, but, but, my brain stammered. I was the kid whose slow learning drove his teacher to distraction, so much so that she humiliated me day in and day out in front of the class. Could it be true? Were my test scores satisfactory—not only satisfactory but quite high? My curiosity was piqued, catapulting me toward my quest for the truth. I had to know. I had to know that I wasn't truly the "class dummy," as I'd believed for so many years.

I requested my school records and discovered that I was actually given IQ tests that third-grade year, not once but twice. The first time, someone who did not know me, whose opinion was unbiased, tested me. I scored so high the administration thought it was a mistake. The second time, a teacher from my school administered the test in place of an independent tester. The score was lower; nonetheless, I placed well into the gifted range.

Realization washed over me like a hot shower, leaving me feeling cleansed and completely exonerated. Now I knew. The reason my teacher was so frustrated with me was because she knew I could learn. She was frustrated because she was not the conduit I needed to learn to read. Realizing that fact, she took it personally, nursed the resentment, and then took it out on me.

Full circle in this sense meant I went the long way around to come back the shortest distance. Once I made a vow that when I was older and bigger, I would look this teacher up and let her experience the pain and humiliation she inflicted on me. I reminded myself many times of that vow, but it was now an empty shell. It had no teeth. My only feelings toward that teacher and all that happened before was empathy. All she did to me was forgiven when Christ forgave me. I learned that unforgiveness destroys the one who can't forgive, not the one who needs forgiveness. It was as simple as that, and I could walk away from the years of hurt and isolation and feeling inadequate. It was all over, it was all done, and I was fine. I had become a stronger person, one who could overcome, endure, and forgive.

That wasn't the end of testing for my ability level, though. I wanted to get into a mechanical drafting class at the local vocational-technical school when I was a high school sophomore. I was to be tested before I could enter the program. My drafting teacher that year said I would never make it through the difficult class.

The thought of being tested again made me feel uncomfortable. My self-confidence at that time was not good. I remember thinking I would be lucky to pass the test and be admitted to the training program I hoped would give me the opportunity to achieve a better life. The testing went forward, my stomach churned the entire time, and I was so afraid to hear the outcome. What if I didn't make it? What if my dream couldn't come true? What if my drafting teacher was right and I couldn't make the grade?

When my test results finally came back, my counselor called me to her office. She seemed disheveled, out of sync, sort of puzzled in fact. I tried to ignore thoughts that I had failed and failed miserably. Was she going to give me the bad news or the good news that I had longed to hear? As I sat before her, trying to muster all of the self-respect and pride that remained within me, I wiped my sweaty palms on my blue jeans. Would she look over the top of her funny little glasses that sat on the end of her nose and say, "Why did you waste my time? You failed the test." Or would she erupt in applause and hang a medal of honor on my chest?

Neither scenario was to be. My high school counselor simply looked up and informed me that among the five high schools in the district, my test score was the highest one. There was no medal, no pomp and circumstance, no fanfare, nothing. She murmured some incoherent statement that made me believe she thought I had somehow pulled off one of the greatest feats of cheating on record. With that, she gestured to the door that I should leave, and she turned back to the work on her desk. As she made no issue of the point, I backed out quietly, closed her door behind me, walked out of the building, and soon thought nothing of the whole incident.

It was to be years later that I realized the weight of her comment about my score. At the time, I was so focused on passing or not passing the test that what she said to me passed by me like a blip on the radar. I didn't comprehend it at the time, and given her casual delivery of the news and her dismissal of me in her office, I thought no more about it. I didn't know there was anything left to think about.

After all, I was the kid held back in grade school; I was the kid beaten up and made an example of by my teacher; I was the kid who came to the conclusion my brain was mush. My counselor's comment to me about being the highest score in five schools, well, I simply passed it off. It was probably a mistake anyway.

The test now passed, I started mechanical drafting class on the first day of my junior year, and completed the course my senior year with honors. I actually secured a job with a local engineering firm during my final year in high school and started my working career.

Life wasn't finished handing me tests. Shortly after my wife and I were married, I applied for a job with the railroad. It was a position as a track laborer, repairing track. I was called to report to the personnel office for testing. When I arrived at the site, I walked into a classroom filled with several hundred people. I understood there were only five open positions. Looking around at the crowd, I thought, *I might as well leave now*, but the testing started before all my courage was gone. So I sat down with the rest of the hopeful applicants and waited.

The test started, and to my dismay, it was a long test and took a long time to complete. Additionally, it was timed, and I watched as so many others turned in their tests long before me. Every time I lifted my eyes, I saw people turning in their tests and leaving the room. As time wore on, I was almost the last person in the room still working on the test. In fact, I was almost the last one to turn in my test. My hopes for this job sank. There was just no way I was going to overcome this to pass this test, just no way, and I wanted it so badly. I had a new wife to provide for; I wanted a home for the two of us. I wanted to make her happy and secure, but I just didn't know how I was going to overcome this new and unwanted challenge and be able to persevere.

We sat in the classroom for what seemed to be an eternity. Waiting for the scoring was agonizing, but it was all done by computer and, actually in the grand scheme of things, did not take long. Restless and unable to sit still, I got up and began to pace. A new person came into the room; I stopped my pacing and stood still to watch what happened next. The new person went to the front and stopped next to the desk near the middle of the classroom. He placed a pile of papers on the desk and then picked up a test from the top of the pile. After a minute, he called out, "Who is Mr. East? Are you here?"

I held up my hand, and he asked me to come to the front of the room. My heart suddenly surged and skipped a beat, then went into double-time and my stomach rumbled, reminding me that I hadn't eaten anything that morning. I felt so conspicuous, as if I were going to be reprimanded for something. My face flushed, and I thought, *What have I done now? I must have really messed something up.* When I reached the table, this guy stared at me long enough to really make me self-conscious. Then he asked, "Why are you applying for this job?"

I was taken aback. I thought for a moment. I wanted this job because I wanted to provide for my wife and future family, be a man, and stand up to my responsibilities. I was no fool, I was no slacker, and I knew it. I wanted to make the best impression I could, and so I stopped and then replied, "I need a job that pays better than the one I have now." He looked at me with curiosity glistening in his eyes. I became unsure, uncomfortable. "Is something wrong?" I asked.

"No, it's just that we have never had anyone score a perfect score on this test. Can you stay and take some more tests today?" he asked. Bewildered, I agreed to stay and take the tests. I wasn't sure what they were looking for, what they wanted from me, but I spent the day taking tests; and when finished, I was told that all of the results were as expected. In the end, I was offered a much higher position than I applied for in the first place.

My eyes were opened, the proverbial scales had dropped away, and now I was growing more and more angry about the things that had happened to me in school. I passed all of the testing for the railroad job with flying colors, with amazing results apparently. How could this happen to someone who was not able to learn, who was not smart? I thought back to my school years. Why had I been treated like the village idiot? If I had a high IQ, why didn't someone tell me that I really had some potential?

The unfortunate side to that experience was I didn't really try to get good grades and did not pursue college because I thought I was not college material. Even I thought I was an idiot. That was what I was led to believe, and as a child, you believe what adults tell you.

Now, it would have been easy to become angry and bitter about my past; however, God was showing me that he had a wonderful life in store for me if I would just accept it, look to the future, and forgive.

There have been many confirmations of my mental ability since, but I will spare you the boring details. All of the lies and confusion that Satan had thrown my way have been dispelled.

The railroad job I was offered, needed, and wanted desperately did not happen. I was fingerprinted and passed a background check. All was well until the railroad doctors reviewed my application; they saw the information about the surgeries on my feet. I became labeled again as a reject. Devastation and despair once again engulfed me, and I once again cried out to God for help. Why was this happening? I apparently had all of the intellectual tools to perform this job well, but now it was gone. I would have to make a living the hard way. The security of a railroad future was not to be.

I did land a better job with a local steel fabrication company in their engineering department. It was not the railroad job, but I made a living.

I had the loving home, the beautiful wife, the beloved family— it was all mine now. It was what I had dreamed of as a youth, what I had longed for on those faraway nights of frigid cold, hanging on the fence while Father went into town. I was no longer hungry, cold, wet, and unloved. The fine dream I'd cherished all those years was reality. But I knew it wasn't over yet.

Satan wanted me dead before I could live out the wonderful life God blessed me with. Satan wanted no one to know what blessings God put on my life. He wanted to negate it all. And I knew he wanted me dead before I could share the good news of Jesus Christ and His life-changing love with others who are just like I was before Christ came into my heart and changed me.

I have been taught to forgive a lot of people who were really difficult to forgive. God has taught that failing to forgive someone destroys the one who cannot forgive, not the one who is unforgiven.

CHAPTER 7

Toby

My thoughts often go back to that life-changing moment when God touched me. I have prayed and begged, even nagged God to just one more time touch me and let me feel the loving warmth of His touch. I longed for it, I begged for just one more touch, just one more moment between Him and me. No response came.

But that doesn't mean God left me alone. Early one morning in my half sleep, God brought me an answer to my prayer: "Before your salvation, your life was cold and without the Spirit. In that moment, you felt the warmth of my love and the Holy Spirit enter your life. Since that time I have always been with you. To recreate that experience for you, I would have to take my hand away; your life would have to go cold and empty again. I would also have to break my promise that I will be with you always."

I totally got the message: to be left without God's presence and his love in my life for even one second would seem to be an eternity. That prayer was never prayed again.

Years drifted by. My family and I went about our daily business. My wife and I were raising our two children, tending to our household. All was well until the day Toby and his family moved in next door to us.

I was twenty-seven years old and had been a Christian for ten years. I had a beautiful wife, son, and daughter. We were buying our first home, and enjoyed our life together as a family. We were happy and proud to be living in our new home, happy in our neighborhood, and active in our church. Life was coming full circle for us. Faith and I began to realize all of our dreams were coming to fruition. We weren't wealthy, but all of our needs were being met. Even with all life's positives, I felt a need for something more: there was that constant yearning for a closer, more intimate relationship with God. I wanted to do something worthwhile for God, and I knew my family would follow my lead. If only I could discover what that path would be. Whatever the path, I knew God would have to lead, open doors, and provide opportunity to be His servant.

Standing at my bedroom window praying after everyone was in bed and the house was quiet, I gazed into the starry evening sky. The magnitude and beauty of God's creation overwhelmed me. My eyes filled with tears to think that someone as insignificant as me could catch the attention of our Creator by whispering a simple prayer. My heart swelled with gratitude at the wonder and glory of God's creation, and at that moment, I felt so close to God, but wanted to be closer. I wanted more knowledge of Him, more closeness, more intimacy.

One evening as I read from the book of Genesis, verse 6:8 caught my attention. It said: "But Noah found grace in the eyes of the Lord." That was it. My spirit acknowledged my longing. I, too, wanted to find grace in the eyes of the Lord.

I began to pray that I might become someone who could do something worthwhile for God.

So caught up in my own mountaintop experience, I scarcely noticed the new neighbors moving in next door.

One evening as our family sat at the dinner table, we heard a child screaming as if the Chain-Saw Murderer was chasing him.

My wife and I ran to the front door to see what was happening. We saw the oldest son of our new neighbors running across the yard. Apparently, his mother sent him for help because his parents were arguing and, subsequently, the father became violent.

Not really wanting to get involved in a domestic squabble, but also fearing for the family's well-being, Faith and I went next door to check and see if our neighbors were okay.

The mother bore no visible bruises, but she was crying and quite upset.

She told us her husband, Toby, was an alcoholic, and they had been separated until he bought the new house next door and promised to dry out. They were supposed to be making a new start, one Toby promised he would stand up and do right by, but unfortunately, he couldn't trim his dependence on alcohol. The new life in the new house hadn't gone quite the way Toby promised it would.

That evening, Toby was late for dinner and when he finally arrived, was drunk and looking to fight.

Faith and I offered a safe place for the mother and her children to stay the night, but she declined, saying that Toby was sleeping and that they would be all right now—no need to worry.

We were surprised to find the next day that the mother and her children had disappeared. The only person remaining in that house was Toby, the alcoholic husband.

While Toby remained in the house, members of a motorcycle gang moved in and took over. The lost family was replaced with friends from a motorcycle gang, proudly displaying tattoos saying, "Sons of Satan."

The family car was kept in the garage. It never moved. Toby's primary mode of transportation became either an old Cadillac hearse or a wicked-looking Harley Davidson chopper.

My family's once peaceful life suddenly turned into sleepless nights and frightening days. On any given night of the week, a party raged all night just a few feet away on the lawn next door. Random people came and went at all hours of the day and night. Trash accumulated on the lawn and in the street. An acrid odor emanated from the property, and when the wind turned in our direction, our house filled with the smell of marijuana smoke. The noise level was unbearable.

My wife and children were too frightened to go out, keeping the doors locked at all times.

We were afraid. We felt as though we were prisoners in our own home. We held no doubts these were the kind of people to avoid, but we didn't dare call the police for fear of retaliation. The tenants and the people coming and going, always high on drugs and alcohol, did nothing to hide the marijuana growing where a vegetable garden once grew.

The man who appeared to be the leader of the gang had a particularly menacing presence. His long brown hair was streaked with oil and dirt. His left cheek was horribly scarred, as if he had been struck with a broken bottle and left to heal without being stitched up. A long, almost black beard hid some of the scar. Thick puffy lips occasionally parted in a hideous smile, which revealed only a few brownish-yellow teeth. To further complement his frightening image, he always wore a black leather vest and blue jeans completely permeated with grease and dirt. Although I was to never know his true name, in my mind, I called him Scarface, and Scarface he remains until this day.

At Scarface's direction, and often his participation, the gang delighted in trying to intimidate us and other neighbors by racing their cycles through our lawns, digging ruts and running over landscaping.

On the outside, I tried to stay calm, but I was afraid, and then, anger began to rise up and overtake me. Who were these people anyway? I prayed about the situation daily, hourly sometimes even; had God not even heard me? Was God not going to reply? Was he going to let this situation continue until our or one of our neighbor's houses was broken into, our loved ones terrorized, maybe even physically harmed? It was enough. Once again, I began to cry out to God. Why was He not doing anything; why was He not interceding on our behalf? I cried out, "Have you heard me at all?" I wanted to be a productive, fruitful Christian and live a productive, fruitful life, at peace in my home and with my family; and instead, I had a motorcycle gang living outside my front door.

We began, as neighbors, to gather in groups to try to devise a plan to rid our neighborhood of the pestilence. None of us knew whether we would be successful, but at least in gathering to talk about it, we grew stronger as neighbors, more attentive to one another, more supportive.

One evening as I tried to repair the damage done to our lawn by the motorcycle tires, the roar of Toby's approaching cycle sent chills up the back of my neck, and my temper passed the boiling point. As he pulled his motorcycle into his driveway, I noticed this time he was alone. Crossing the drive before he had time to dismount, I yelled, "If you or any of your friends harm my family, you'll have to deal with me—one on one."

His response was unexpected: Toby sat back on the seat of the bike, his dirty hands folded in his lap, surprisingly subdued as I threatened him.

His eyes met mine and did not waver, but his reaction to me was different than ever before.

The abrasive exterior was broken down. As I stared into his eyes, I found I was looking into a deep well of sadness and discontent. I wanted to maintain my momentum and anger so I tried to avoid looking him in the eyes, but it was no use. The well was deep and full, and it was pulling me in. Something in my brain registered. Toby's eyes were blue. I never noticed that before.

Something deep behind his eyes was imploring me, no, yelling, "Help me, please help me. I need something I just can't seem to find."

Astounded and worn out, I dropped my threats and backed into my house. I locked the door behind me, gasping for air. Whatever had just happened between Toby and me, well, I just didn't understand it. Looking into his eyes, I would have imagined I would find a black, tarry presence, and instead, what I found was a lostness I had not seen before in any person. That man, Toby, was suddenly a real person to me, and it was a disturbing revelation. What was I to do with it? What would God have me do with it?

My mind was active, and as I undressed for bed, I wondered if sleep would elude me that night. Keyed up, I decided to get up and pray for a while.

That night, Toby was in my prayers as usual; however this time, the look in his eyes haunted me. Scriptures ran through my mind like Matthew 22:39: "You shall love your neighbor as yourself." And Matthew 5:44: "But I say to you, love your enemies, bless those who curse you, do good to those who hate you, and pray for those who spitefully use you and persecute you."

Something was coming home to me. For days, I had prayed not for Toby, or Scarface, or for any of the gang members, but about them. Reality wiggled its finger in my face and said, "You are a Christian, and you of all people should know better." I began to understand. My viewpoint all along was in error. I was praying for deliverance from a problem, not for someone who needed

Christ in his life. As a Christian, I should have known better. I felt foolish, ashamed, and confused. A bitter conflict raged within me, spoiling the wonderful joy I was experiencing. One side of me was crying out fear and hate, while the other side was whispering, showing compassion. Which way to turn? The fork in the road stood before me, and I would have to choose which direction I would take very soon.

I had been reading in Romans and discovered Romans 10:14-15:

> How then shall they call on Him in whom they have not believed? And how shall they believe in Him of whom they have not heard? And how shall they hear without a preacher? And how shall they preach unless they are sent? As it is written:
>
> "How beautiful are the feet of those who preach the gospel of peace, who bring glad tidings of good things!"

That settled it for me; I knew my decision was made. I would have to stand face to face with Toby and the gang I feared.

One Saturday afternoon, I was standing on a ladder, painting our house. The usual party crowd began to gather next door. A motorcycle raced through our already abused lawn, and loud music mixed with obscene language irritated my tightly coiled nerves. Again with this, I began to see. *When will they leave us alone?*

In a split second, God spoke to my heart. "Now is the time; he needs to find the same peace you have found."

"Why me?" I argued, still on the ladder. "Why now, with all those bikers there?"

I could have argued all day long, but it was senseless and I knew it would be. The power of God's will took control. Suddenly

I was off the ladder, my paint bucket and brush left behind, and I found myself standing in the midst of a crowd that would frighten an NFL defensive lineman or a professional wrestler. I heard Scarface say, "Don't worry, Toby. I'll take care of him."

But their eyes couldn't see that I was not alone.

I stood face to face with Toby.

Just as God guided my feet in those moments, He gave me the words to say: "Toby, these people aren't your friends. You know, the best friend I ever had told me how to find peace with God, and I want to be your best friend." I reached out to shake his hand, only I didn't let go until I had explained just how Christ could turn his life around and fill his life with joy.

The crowd stood back, silent, immobile. Toby and I talked for nearly an hour about the love of Christ. It seemed to be the first time anyone talked to Toby about Christ and salvation, but the tough exterior would not allow the love of God to come into his heart. Before walking away, I asked him to call me anytime he felt the need to talk.

Back inside my house, it dawned on me—the party broke up while Toby and I talked, and the bikers vanished. We never saw them again.

What was this thing that happened to me? It was so unlike anything I had ever done before—or even thought I was capable of doing. For me to have faced down a crowd of rough motorcycle riders and minister to Toby stunned me. God must have engineered it, because I could not have done it on my own.

My wife overheard Toby and I talking outside. She was in tears, staring at me as if I had become something supernatural. For some time, we could only look at each other in dismay. We knew beyond a shadow of a doubt that for a few moments, God had taken complete control of my mind and body.

Some weeks later, my wife and I noticed Toby hobbling around the yard with one leg and one arm in casts. We noticed tape around his ribs and cuts and bruises on all exposed skin.

One of our neighbors later told us Toby was almost killed in a recent automobile accident.

Once again, my heart became burdened. It was clear to me God was dealing with Toby. The next time I saw him in his yard, I approached him again to talk. Toby hobbled back through his front door and slammed it in my face.

With the slam of the door, the burden was gone, and the look in his eyes haunted me no more.

Sullen, gray clouds spattered blobs of rain on my windshield as I drove home from work, just days later on a cold December afternoon. As I turned down our street, I recognized blood red lights pulsating like an open artery from near our house. Instantly, terror sent horrible thoughts racing through my mind.

As I pulled into my driveway, I saw an ambulance backed up in Toby's drive; EMTs were shutting the heavy back doors. Our front door was open, and I found the living room filled with Toby's grief-stricken family members, grieving from the horror of finding him dead.

He had been dead for two days. An overdose of drugs and alcohol had ended his life.

Learning of Toby's death, I felt my face pale. I felt weak. Toby was gone. There was no chance to speak to him, to show him the love of Christ, to open his eyes to the weary path he was on. What I felt for Toby was more than just a feeling of responsibility and compassion for my neighbor; God brought the two of us together for a very important reason. I could only hope that in his last dying moments, Toby might have cried out to God, remembered something I said to him in our last conversation, and surrendered his life and soul to God.

That night, I once again stood at my bedroom window— only this time, I was praying for forgiveness. How could I ever question God's will again? After all, His love is there for everyone, regardless of our present condition.

I often think back on that experience, and to this day, the way God answered my prayer awes me. He used me in a way I was not expecting. He used me in His way, not mine.

This experience was clearly of God, not something imagined or contrived.

CHAPTER 8

A Nun on the Plane

J ust a few months after the death of my neighbor Toby, my company sent me to Pasadena, California, to negotiate the contract for a very large project.

The steel fabrication company I worked for needed this project badly; I would have to step up and take the lead.

It would be my first time in a plane, and the idea of being in the air was disturbing. At age twenty-eight, all of my travel had taken place behind the wheel of my own car. Putting my life in the hands of someone I didn't know made me very uncomfortable.

Proposals were written and sent to our prospective customer, and we were close enough to reach an agreement. The deal was almost done, and my departure date was drawing near. One day, I expressed my apprehension with air travel to my coworkers. One of them said, "Don't worry about that. Just get on the plane and find a nun to sit by; you'll be fine." Such an odd comment, it didn't seem to mean anything, and so I blew it off. Until my return trip, that is.

My flight itinerary took me from Springfield to Denver, and then Denver to Los Angeles and then to Pasadena by shuttle bus. The return trip was just the reverse of the trip out.

The trip going out to Pasadena was actually pleasant and uneventful. After successfully completing the negotiations for the new project and reaching a satisfactory agreement with the customer, I began my journey back to Springfield.

I will never forget what happened next. Boarding the plane for the trip from Los Angeles to Denver, I was walking down the narrow aisle between the seats looking at my seat assignment on the boarding pass. I was counting down the rows of seats, and as I found my assigned seat, there seated next to me was a nun in full habit.

Suddenly my coworker's comment about sitting next to a nun came back to me, and I started laughing. Not wanting the nun to think I was laughing at her, I sat down and told her the story, and luckily, she appreciated it. In the end, we enjoyed a good laugh. Relaxed, we absorbed ourselves in our own business as the flight took off; she reading a mystery book and me looking out the window from time to time, anticipating my arrival home. It had been a grueling three days, with nonstop negotiations until late in the day before my return trip home.

The flight was smooth until we reached the mountains just before Denver. Suddenly, crossing over the mountains, we experienced the worst turbulence I've ever been through. My companion dropped her book and scrambled to find it under the seat. I watched the clouds rise and fall through the window, wondering if this was normal and how we were going to get through this new situation.

Momentarily the pilot announced over the intercom that a previous flight had some injured passengers because of the rough and unexpected turbulence.

The nun put her book aside, leaned over, and commented she took my story to be humorous until we hit the turbulence. Fortunately, it didn't last long, and we landed in Denver on time.

"God knows our path ahead and the end of our journey," she said, and she gave me a blessing as we departed the plane. Once in the terminal, she told me she had never had a more interesting flight, and we wished each other well as we parted.

I never knew the nun's name; I never asked it, and she didn't ask my name either. Was our encounter just coincidence, was He just messing with me, or was He reassuring me of His presence during rough times?

In retrospect, I still reflect and still wonder about it, but I do know that God is indeed with us; especially during the storms of life, He is our shelter.

As it says in Matthew 28:20: "Teaching them to observe all things that I have commanded you; and lo, I am with you always, even to the end of the age."

CHAPTER 9

Teaching Class

Several years passed with no real godlike direction in my life, no option to minister to anyone, and I began to wonder if God would use me again to impact the life of someone looking to find his or her way.

The years were adding up all too quickly, and I began to think that God just was never going to give me another chance. Maybe I was too old. Maybe He had forgotten me. In the past, when He called, I heard Him and obeyed, even the tough assignments.

I felt like the young athlete begging the coach, "Put me in, coach. I am ready to play." I was begging God daily to bring me an opportunity to minister to someone, to make a difference in someone's life, and I heard nothing back. Once again, I felt confused, conflicted, not sure whether I was part of God's plan or not. However, God in His supreme wisdom knows and has a plan.

I began teaching a Bible class for men my own age on Sunday morning, filling in for the usual teacher who was suddenly very sick. While studying for the upcoming lesson, I felt as though I were not getting the full meaning of the scriptures I was reading, that there was more. I began to pray that God would make the scriptures come to life for me; I needed a better and deeper understanding of the message God was trying to give me. Early the next morning, the Holy Spirit awakened me and said,

"The Bible is like the body of Christ or the broken bread in the Holy Communion. The Holy Spirit is like the blood of Christ or the wine in the Holy Communion. The body cannot live without the blood. The Word cannot live without the Holy Spirit. Always pray for the Holy Spirit to guide you when studying the Word, and it will come to life for you."

Astounded, I repeated the Holy Spirit's words and committed those words to memory. My internal cup was running over; the weight of this incredible blessing washed over me. Wisdom, wisdom far beyond any perception of wisdom I knew previously but certainly in accordance with God's Word, was now mine. My measure in knowing these experiences come from God is simple. First, knowledge I did not previously possess comes; second, the information is in accordance with the Word of God.

This rule of thumb is my guide. It was then, it is now, and it always will be.

CHAPTER 10

My Mother's Passing

My mother passed away on June 21, 2006, the first official day of summer; and upon her passing, I lost, not only my beloved mother, but also the woman who set my feet on a path destined for glory. We were practicing Methodists, or at least Mother was, and I remember her taking us kids to church every Sunday no matter how tired she was or how inventive she had to be to get it done. She took us to Sunday school and church. Often we had to catch a city bus and ride across town to our home church, the Campbell Avenue Methodist Church.

It was Mom and us kids. My father did not attend, except on rare occasions. He did not make it easy for us to get to Sunday school and church. He was either sleeping at home, or he was gone and we didn't know where.

My mother laid the foundation stones for my spiritual life and cultivated growth in my faith through her actions and prayers. Her faith was legendary. She had the resolve of Job in the Bible, faith unwavering, and patience, and was always looking ahead.

She was an attractive woman, but she was faithful to my father, even though, as I knew, other men tried to get her attention, flirting with her when she was working or elsewhere, when we were out. Although she was kind to them, she never responded to their advances.

Her life was difficult and hard, and I could not understand how she lived with that, how she coped, or why she lived with the misery, why she didn't just get out. She could have had so much more, as I imagined from the number of men who wanted to talk to her, but exchanging one life for another didn't seem to be her ideal. Her first husband, my father, was abusive and seemed to take pleasure in being unkind to her. He would disappear for days, and no one knew where he went. As a child, I remember hearing Mother ask him where he had been the night before or the day before, and he would just reply, "That is for me to know and you to find out."

Mother stayed with my father until all three children were old enough to be somewhat independent. We were all in high school or already graduated when she finally left him and got a divorce.

In time, Mother married again. Her second husband was not much better than the first husband. Ralph was only interested in having a caretaker, and he saw an easy target with my mother. Mother had forgotten how to ask for what she wanted and needed. She was getting on in years, and the security of a husband who could provide a home and the basic needs to sustain life became appealing to her—and by basic needs of life, I do mean basic. Mother didn't realize that until after a few years of marriage to Ralph.

It was quickly apparent the marriage was one of convenience, for both of them for different reasons. After a few years, the lack of caring for one another was noticeable. My sisters and I commented on it, but none of us wanted to interfere or cause trouble for Mother. We talked about it sometimes, and then we didn't talk about it, and then the issue would flare up again and we would talk about it. But we never did anything about what we saw and what we felt.

Mother had been plagued with several critical illnesses throughout her life. She had rheumatic fever as a teenager. Rheumatic fever is an inflammatory disease that may develop after an infection with group A Streptococcus bacteria, such as strep throat or scarlet fever. The disease can affect the heart, joints, skin, and brain. Recovery from this disease was slow and arduous in 1941. The disease was no doubt the result of an untreated case of strep throat.

In 1955, she attempted suicide, as discussed in chapter one. When I was a teenager in 1965, she had a hysterectomy and developed a blood-clotting problem. She had several blood clots in her lungs and almost died. After she remarried in 1994, her colon ruptured, causing gangrene and peritonitis. Somehow she survived four major surgeries to repair the damage and trauma of having her colon spliced back together.

The last time she became ill was in 2004, when she had a stroke and lost her ability to walk and get around. With this latest illness, she had to go into a nursing home.

The bills for her hospital stay and the nursing home became quite a point of conflict between Ralph, his family, and me. Mom had a small amount of money put aside to cover her funeral expenses; it was such a small sum that it was not enough to cover her final costs, but Ralph and his family felt that I should use this money to pay her medical bills. When Mother went into the nursing home, I went to the Day Funeral Home in Marshfield, Missouri, and prearranged her funeral. I knew that the money she had was not enough. Faith and I made up the difference. At her death, Ralph did have a twinge of conscience and agreed to pay a small amount on the headstone. If I had not fought so hard to preserve this money as I did, I cannot imagine what the outcome would have been. Mom insisted that I not spend any of my own money for this purpose, but I refused to scrimp on her funeral; I wanted to honor her, and I gladly did so.

I was alone in my concern and care for her. Both of my sisters married and moved to the Kansas City area. They were busy with their lives, and we did not communicate much. I was here; they were there. Mother was here, and she needed care. She needed someone to manage her health care and other needs, and so, being the child who was present, that responsibility fell on me. I was happy to see that she was cared for.

At some point after she was ensconced in the nursing home, Mother asked Faith and me to go to her house and bring back some clothes for her to use in the nursing home. She specifically asked for clothing Faith and I bought her during a hospital stay some ten years prior.

Faith and I did as requested, going through her closet to find the clothing items she asked us to bring to her. At her house as I was shoving my hands through the myriad of hangers and clothing in her closet, I became incensed when I saw the condition of all of her clothing. Every single garment was completely worn out and threadbare. I could only find a few items in acceptable condition. I was appalled, and as Faith and I gazed at each other in astonishment, we mentally joined in a decision.

Putting the clothing aside and closing the door to Mother's closet, Faith and I quietly walked out the front door, saying nothing to each other, and drove to the nearest clothing store. There was no way either of us would have allowed my mother to wear the worn, worthless clothing left in her closet. We knew what we needed to do. Quickly we marched through the women's clothing area, pulling clothing out, looking all of it over, choosing what we would provide Mother with, and then we advanced to the checkout and bought her a new wardrobe.

I sometimes wanted to scream at my sisters, "Did you not know? Did you not see how she was living? You are so busy living your lives, being selfish, did you not see how our mother suffered, what her life was really like?" But I never said any of those things to my sisters. I couldn't and I wouldn't. After all, I didn't see it either. Mom told me that Ralph only let her have one new dress each year, on her birthday. When we came to visit, she would be wearing her birthday dress. It took us years before we noticed it was always the same dress.

What I did was take care of the things I could take care of regarding my mother. And I will leave it at that and not expand any further in an effort to spare the feelings of those who didn't share in the experience.

As Mother drew her last breath, I saw a vision of her walking the streets of pure gold in heaven and knew that her tears would flow no more. I knew that she would be singing with the angels and waiting for me there.

Once the funeral and the stress of caring for my mother as her health slowly eroded were over, I began praying God would show me why such a faithful person would be caused to suffer such a difficult life.

It was not long before the answer came, and it came in a curt reply.

I do my best praying at 3:00 a.m., it seems, and two days after the funeral, the Holy Spirit said, "I can't believe you have not reasoned this out for yourself, but here it is." He then gave me these scriptures:

> Then his wife said to him, "Do you still hold fast to your integrity? Curse God and die!"
> But he said to her, "You speak as one of the foolish women speaks. Shall we indeed accept good from

God, and shall we not accept adversity?" In all this,
Job did not sin with his lips (Job 2:9-10).

Blessed is the man who endures temptation; for
when he has been approved, he will receive the crown
of life, which the Lord has promised to those who love
Him (James 1:12).

The Holy Spirit entered my mind and whispered, "This is
what was required of her to win her crown in glory."

The scriptures the Holy Spirit gave me are engraved on
Mother's headstone. I know when we see each other in heaven,
she will be wearing her brilliant, jewel-encrusted crown.

Because she loved them so much, we asked for and received
permission from the Gruelle family to engrave on her headstone
Raggedy Ann and Andy.

Through all of her trials and hardship, she never blamed
anyone else and certainly never questioned God.

CHAPTER 11

Something Evil

There's an old saying, "Something wicked this way comes," and on July 15, 2010, Faith and I called 911 and had her father taken to the hospital. He took a bad fall the day before, and in the ensuing hours, gradually lost his ability to stand or walk.

It troubled us to watch a loved one experience this kind of difficulty, especially because he was ninety years old and took great pride in his independence. But Faith and I sensed that at the age of ninety, the end was drawing near. We were not ready to say good-bye to our last remaining parent, regardless of the assurance that he was a born-again Christian and a fervent believer.

Many long hours were spent sitting in the emergency room, and later when he was admitted into his hospital room, we remained to help in any way we could.

An MRI revealed that the first time he fell, he suffered a concussion and a subdural hematoma, or a brain bleed. It was a serious diagnosis and a frightening one. We stayed on at the hospital until we were spent and Dad was calm and comfortable.

Faith and I finally got some rest the evening of July 17, and it was a deep sleep, coming hard and fast. Sometime around three o'clock in the morning, I awakened with the odd sensation of someone standing over me. Terror crawled up my spine and into my heart. Something extremely evil stood at the side of my bed and was standing over me. It was shocking—an evil of such magnitude that I actually smelled it and tasted it. The smell and taste was unlike anything I had ever experienced in my entire life.

Somehow, heart pounding, I opened my eyes and saw nothing but the reassuring lines of my bedroom. The sensation lasted only a few seconds and vanished as soon as I heard the familiar voice of the Holy Spirit say, "You have no reason to fear him, and you are mine."

I don't remember asking the question before the answer came. Perhaps the Holy Spirit knew I would be wondering just what that awful, evil thing was.

The Holy Spirit told me a higher demon had come to me, and there were a much smaller number of higher demons than lesser demons. The Holy Spirit told me millions of lesser demons exist, capable of instigating sin and evil, but the higher demons are capable of much greater sin and evil. The Holy Spirit told me to fear nothing the future held. In the face of the great storms that lay ahead, I was to set my jaw against the wind and not waver from my faith.

I was told that I was to praise God the Father and Christ the Son in all that would happen to me. I was told to constantly be in a spirit of praise, for this pleases God. Demons, both higher and lower, hate to hear Christians praising the Father, Son, and Holy Spirit. When they sense someone in the spirit of praise, they cower and flee immediately.

Before the Holy Spirit left me, He told me that my father-in-law would not live long, that now was his time and he would be going home very soon.

As I wept in the spirit, I filled up with the spirit and power of something truly wonderful and supernatural. I was so overcome by it that I cried out, waking my wife.

As soon as the Holy Spirit left me, I began to relate to her what had just happened to me. At the time, I wasn't sure whether she believed me or was moved in any way by my encounter with the Holy Spirit. When her father passed easily from this life to the next on Sunday, July 18, I knew she understood. We knew my encounter with the Holy Spirit was genuine and not to be taken lightly.

I learned an extremely valuable lesson from the words of the Holy Spirit. If you want protection from the evil that is in the world, be constantly in a spirit of praise, and the demons, both higher and lower, will flee from you.

We laid him to rest after a long life well-lived on Tuesday, July 27, 2010, in Maple Park Cemetery, Aurora, Missouri. It was a military funeral because of his proud service to his country during World War II.

We will see you soon, Pops.

Chapter 12

The Illness

Throughout the years, I have experienced so many encounters with the Holy Spirit that to recite all of them would fill another book, so I have related just a few in the previous chapters. The latest and most significant event between the Holy Spirit and me began on Sunday, December 16, 2012.

That particular Sunday, it was my turn to teach the Bible lesson to our small married-adult group at our home church, Ridgecrest Baptist Church.

Unfortunately, I wasn't feeling my best that morning and was suffering with what I thought was a sinus infection, but I went on to Sunday school and taught the lesson. My lesson topic was about putting on the full armor of God by living a life of righteousness.

"Put on the whole armor of God, that you may be able to stand against the wiles of the devil" (Eph. 6:11).

Here I was, standing before the class with an obvious ailment. I stood there preaching about having the full protection from the wiles of the Devil, and I was so obviously ill. Could I have looked any sillier? Nonetheless, as soon as I finished the lesson, I drove to urgent care. My whole head was throbbing; I was feverish, sweating, chilled, sick to my stomach.

Now, is this being protected from the wiles of the Devil? I felt worse than bad.

The urgent care doctor prescribed a breathing treatment and some antibiotics. I returned home and began treatment in hopes of returning to health quickly. The Christmas season was upon us, and we were going to be busy with church, parties, and family events. Enjoying Christmas with my family and friends was important to me, and I diligently took the prescribed treatment.

The treatment seemed to be working for almost a week. I breathed a sigh of relief and pleasure and went about my business: Christmas shopping, wrapping packages, doing all of the things Faith and I and our family enjoyed during the Christmas season. I was looking forward to 2013 and to what it might bring for my family and me. It was a happy, joyful time, and I enjoyed every minute of it.

December 23, 2012, began in a most unremarkable way, as we were busy with plans and preparations for our Christmas. Faith and I had dinner and went for our usual two-mile walk around seven o'clock, but something was off for me. I couldn't make the whole walk, and when we reached the halfway point, I began feeling somewhat winded, just a little out of breath and weak. "Faith," I said as I braced my hand on one knee and panted, "Faith, I'm feeling winded. I need to go back home."

"Okay, we can do that," she said, and turned me around for home.

I saw the question in her eyes, but I wasn't ready to contemplate that yet. All I knew was that I wasn't feeling up to par on the walk and I wasn't sure why.

Once we reached home, I became more and more uncomfortable, and my heart rate skyrocketed. I knew when I felt this way, the usual problem was my blood sugar had dropped below 80. What I had to do to relieve the problem was eat something to bring it back up to 90 or above.

I have been a diabetic since 1999, and I am well-acquainted with what works for me when it comes to managing my blood sugar levels. So on this night, after checking my blood, I discovered my blood sugar levels were not the problem, and so I was bewildered about what was happening to me.

Later in the evening, I could not seem to get my breath; I was beginning to struggle to breathe. By bedtime, I was moving from the bed to the recliner to pacing the floor as I tried to find comfort and some form of relief. Breathing was difficult, almost impossible. I was also coughing uncontrollably and spitting up that horrible army green junk in great gobs. I discovered I could stand over the bathroom sink, with both hands spread apart, my palms facedown on the countertop, bent at the waist in a tripod position, feet together flat on the floor, and I could breathe a little better. This position seemed to give some relief, but it was only temporary. I finally gave in to my wife and agreed to go to St. John's Regional Hospital, or as we know it now, Mercy Hospital Emergency Room, and seek medical attention.

It was late at night. I was tired, Faith was tired, and we were worn soldiers. Arriving at the ER, we saw the place was crowded with people in every state of medical need. I hated being there, and it seemed everyone in the waiting room needed help more than me.

The florescent lights glared in our faces. There was an unsung sound of constant need and an odor of human that bothered me. As I stared around the ER reception area, I saw little children, sick, suffering with flulike symptoms, their mothers sitting nearby, looking disheveled and anxious. Here I was a grown man with some kind of malady, but still, I felt selfish and self-indulgent when I gazed upon their tiny fever-ridden faces and heard them cry to their mothers. I was hurt by what I saw. I wished I didn't have to be there, taking up the doctors' time, but I knew I was in some kind of trouble and I was starting to panic.

Minutes ticked by. My air passageways were closing even further. By the time medical care was offered to me, I was desperate for some help. I didn't understand why I was so sick and not getting any better. In the back of my mind, I began to wonder if some malicious force might be trying to kill me.

CHAPTER 13

The Fight Begins

I sat on the ER table under a bright light. The medical team checked my ears, eyes, throat, heartbeat, lungs, and every other preliminary checking they needed to do. They then left me alone, assuring me the doctor on call would be in shortly. More minutes ticked by as I sat there, struggling to breathe. Finally, the ER doctor pulled back the curtain. After checking my chart and reassuring me that everything would be fine, he ordered blood work, a chest X-ray, and several tests, along with a breathing treatment. The tests came back indicating nothing was wrong with me; the breathing treatment opened up my air passages, giving me some relief.

Because the tests failed to reveal any pneumonia or infections, the ER doctor released me into Faith's care, sending us home with several prescriptions for antibiotics and an inhaler. With his hand on my shoulder, the doctor declared he believed my malady to be some kind of "community-acquired pneumonia." I had never heard of such a thing, but he was the one with the medical degree. I would be compliant.

The prescribed antibiotics and inhaler now in my system, I began to try to rest but found it useless. By early Christmas Eve morning, I was simply unable to breathe. It would be another trip to the emergency room.

Faith made the unenviable phone calls to our children calling off our Christmas celebration until a later date and hustled me into the car.

This time at the ER, we insisted that the doctor notify my internist, Dr. Froncek, of my condition, which they did, and Dr. Froncek answered promptly. He had me admitted and ordered a host of new tests.

The hours that followed were torturous. Test after test was ordered and conducted. I could not stand erect, sit in a chair, or lie flat. In order to get any air into my lungs at all, I had to stand in the tripod position so that I could take in enough oxygen to remain conscious.

For hours, I stood there, gasping for air, my heart rate elevated, and there was no rest until sometime late Christmas evening. It was excruciating, exhausting, and painful on every level.

At some point, I told the nursing staff, "I cannot continue in this condition, I am running out of strength. I can't do this much longer."

My heart rate was nearly double my normal resting rate and had been doubled for almost forty-eight hours. During all that time, I had not rested or slept. I was running on serious empty, just no strength left. I finally collapsed with exhaustion. My marathon was over. There was nothing left.

CHAPTER 14

The Rapid-Response Team

When I collapsed, I went into respiratory arrest. My blood pressure reached stroke levels, and my body temperature tapped out at 104 degrees. As if that weren't enough, I also went into septic shock, and my white blood cell count rose above 40,000. I did not know any of this, as I was unconscious and things of this world were not a part of my memory.

My daughter, a nurse in the oncology department of Mercy Hospital, came into my room as I lapsed into unconsciousness. She saw my mouth turn blue and my eyes roll back in my head. Being a nurse, she knew the ramifications of a 78 blood oxygen level.

Immediately, she ran to the nursing station. "If you don't call the rapid-response team, I will," she snapped at the charge nurse. "Do it! Do it now!"

The problem was, at this point, my doctors did not have a clue as to what was causing my respiratory problems. All blood cultures, X-rays, CT scans, EKGs, spinal tap, and many other tests revealed nothing, so a treatment plan could not be established.

At the same time, I was rapidly declining into a death spiral, and no one recognized it. The rapid-response team arrived. I was moved to the cardio intensive care unit on the fourth floor of Mercy Hospital.

Dr. Patel, the intensive care doctor who was on duty at the time, used a bronchoscope to get a look inside my lungs. He found that they were filled with mucus plugs, which almost completely cut off all airflow. He suctioned out as much of the restricting mucus plugs as he could.

I learned about mucus plugs as a result of all this. Mucus plugs are a fleshlike material that does not show up in an X-ray or CAT scan. Mucus plugs resemble the pink slime found in meat products, as reported in recent news articles. They are gross, slimy, and invasive, almost alien, and all this was in my lungs!

Once the mucus plugs were discovered and suctioned out of my lungs, my condition began to slowly improve.

My body was being kept alive by machines and medications, but my soul had slipped away. How long I was gone and exactly when it happened, I do not know, but I was gone.

CHAPTER 15

---※◦◦※---

The City of Light
(New Jerusalem, Heaven)

"Then I, John, saw the holy city, New Jerusalem, coming down out of heaven from God, prepared as a bride adorned for her husband" (Rev. 21:2).

While the CICU doctors and nursing staff fought desperately to save my life, I was witnessing firsthand the glory of heaven.

To say this experience was amazing is a weak understatement. Nothing so powerful, so beautiful, so meaningful has happened to me before or after. I was filled with a sense of knowing.

I knew exactly where I was and what had happened to my old body. The Holy Spirit was coaching me every inch of the way.

The Holy Spirit told me I was on the other side of the threshold in heaven, my old body had passed, and I now had a new, perfect body.

Planet earth and the things of that world were becoming a distant memory.

I saw what I called at the time the City of Light. I was corrected in mid-thought; this was the New Jerusalem or the City of Heaven. It was the dwelling place of God.

Complete joy washed over me, a joy unimagined. I felt free, unfettered, and completely aware of the world and universe and everything around me. I felt no worry, no rush; and most of all, a feeling of wellness, complete wellness, filled me.

I was communicating with the Holy Spirit, and information was simply given to me, one spirit to another. There was no audible voice of great authority as you might imagine.

I could think for myself, and I seemed to have a free will.

There was a horizon, and off in the far distance was this beautiful city radiating with brilliant light, more beautiful than I can explain.

The light radiating from the city was made up of brilliant pastel colors, similar to neon but much more brilliant, like nothing here on earth. The light seemed to be predominately yellow.

The city was so beautiful, so radiant, such a positive light flow, and I remember thinking, *how beautiful—how can this be?* I was immediately told while I was in mid-thought that Jesus was the light. He was pure perfection, and the light was pure and perfect.

It was drawing me closer, and I knew where I was: I was on my way to the City of Heaven. I had arrived, my race had been run, and my journey was almost over. I was being drawn forward toward the city.

I did not feel as if I were being escorted by anyone or anything, but was aware that I was progressing onward toward the city.

I remember looking for the gates to the City of Heaven, but could not make out anything that looked like a gate or an entrance. I was too far away.

I remember the first time I saw the Rocky Mountains and recall how close they looked from so far away. We drove for hours before we actually reached the foothills and base of the mountains.

My wife gave me a gift of a hot air balloon ride for my birthday several years before, and the movement experienced during that ride was similar to my trip toward the City of Light. You are moving along without any sensation of movement, just a gentle float in the direction of a light breeze.

By nature, I tend to be impatient, and this occasion was proving to be typical. I wanted to get to the city faster. The Holy Spirit either read my mind again or sensed my feelings because I was not aware of any thoughts of impatience. Again, I was coached about time. The Spirit said, "There is no time or anything to mark the passing of time in heaven."

This comment was entirely preemptive and without warning.

I was so amazed by the wisdom and mind reading of my personal coach; it was like you didn't even need to think. A person could become so lazy and dependent.

> For behold,
> He who forms mountains,
> And creates the wind,
> Who declares to man what his thought *is,*
> And makes the morning darkness,
> Who treads the high places of the earth—
> The LORD God of hosts *is* His name (Amos 4:13).

CHAPTER 16

A Chorus of Prayer

> So there was great joy in Jerusalem, for since the time
> of Solomon the son of David, king of Israel, there had
> been nothing like this in Jerusalem. Then the priests,
> the Levites, arose and blessed the people, and their
> voice was heard; and their prayer came up to His holy
> dwelling place, to heaven (2 Chron. 30:26-27).

A huge chorus of prayer began to reach me. Voices, hundreds of thousands of voices, joined together until I thought I was hearing one big roar. It was impossible to hear any one voice because there were thousands of prayers making their way toward the city.

I heard different pitches, male, female, young, old, all languages, many weeping in the spirit as they prayed, but they all prayed with great conviction from their hearts.

As the sound intensified, I struggled to hear but could only catch a word now and then. Some were moving toward the city at the same pace as I. Some were slower and others faster, but the prayers were moving constantly toward the city in untold numbers.

The Holy Spirit came to me again. "These are the prayers of the saints still on earth. A great number of people are praying for you in this very moment."

So many people believe that prayer is redundant and that God's will ultimately prevails, so why pray? God's will always prevails; however, it is so important to pray. I am convinced that if no one had been praying for me on December 25, 2012, I would not be writing this story today. I have to believe that our prayers can change the will of God. If prayer were not important to God, why did I hear so many prayers radiating toward heaven?

Pray and praise God always in all things. Pray from your heart and ask for your needs to be met. Praise the one and only God of the universe, the God of Abraham, Isaac, and Jacob.

CHAPTER 17

Heavenly Bliss and Joy
Beyond Imagination

Drifting in a state of limbo, I was enveloped in an incredible state of comfort and serenity. My physical suffering and all of my heartaches and struggles of the world from which I had just come were at an end.

In this heightened state of being, I sensed my body was new and perfect, completely free of any defect; my sinful nature was gone, diabetes and the illness I had just died of were gone, and none of those things were holding me down any longer. In fact, I no longer needed the armor of God because I did not need to be concerned about Satan and his onslaught of constant attacks on my health, my spiritual life, my family, or any other facet of my life on earth.

I would never again be in pain of any kind, and there would be no more need for medical tests.

I was in heaven, a place where Satan would never be, a place where he had no power or presence.

As I was moving, I realized I had no physical pain. Death completely lost its hold on me forever; I would never have to face the thought of death again. There was no need to fear anything because I was safe in the arms of my Savior, Jesus Christ.

Fear is a tool of the Devil; since the Devil and his influence are not possible in heaven, all fear was gone.

What I was experiencing was so glorious that to try to describe it would be a waste of time. Human words cannot adequately and completely describe such joy as this; experience is the only teacher.

"The fear of man brings a snare but whoever trusts in the Lord shall be safe" (Prov. 29:25).

"But in keeping with his promise we are looking forward to a new heaven and a new earth, where righteousness dwells" (2 Peter 3:13).

CHAPTER 18

A Revelation

"Therefore, just as through one man's sin entered the world, and death through sin, and thus death spread to all men, because all sinned" (Rom. 5:12).

The revelation following this narration came to me, brought by the Holy Spirit, an invisible presence, an all-knowing manifestation, one who knew my every thought. Once an idea occurred to me, or a question, or something I was wondering about, the answer would come to me mentally. It was immediate; although quiet but solid, the authority was undeniable.

It was a comforting presence. I was happy because I did not have to wonder about anything. The Holy Spirit would occur in thought, and all would be explained. There was no limit, so far as I could tell, to this knowingness.

As I traveled through the expanse of heaven, somewhere far away from earth, the contrast between the two was so radically different because earth is a place affected by sin. Sickness, death, poverty, and crime are simply in every aspect of life on earth. Selfishness rules, as human beings push everyone out of the way, charging ahead for their own gain. I've heard of an old phrase that really sums up the totality of earth: "Get all you can, can all you can sit on the can, and destroy the rest."

After knowing earth and its rhythms for so long, I wondered about and looked forward to heaven—that place of great love, peace, joy, and contentment.

In my earth life, I knew heaven is what God intended our life to be like on earth. In the garden of Eden, before Adam and Eve committed the original sin, life was as it is in heaven. Satan changed it all when he convinced Adam and Eve to disobey God. They ate of the Tree of Knowledge of Good and Evil, and the whole game changed; it changed for every generation to come after them. It was Satan who brought upon us sickness, suffering, heartbreak, and death.

Humankind is not guiltless either, however; as easy and convenient as it might be to lay the blame for the fall of humans solely at Satan's feet, the humans willingly took part. Once humankind became aware of evil and was able to achieve evil, humankind would eventually be destroyed.

Another tree mentioned in and often overlooked by many who read the book of Genesis is the Tree of Life. Humans could have eaten of the Tree of Life after acquiring the capability for evil and lived forever, becoming more and more evil as time passed and thus capable of great evil.

In the end, God was forced to expel humankind from the garden and put a limit on his life expectancy.

Can you imagine someone as evil as Adolf Hitler, as evil as he was, living for all eternity and becoming more and more evil? I can't.

Not just Adolf Hitler, but many others acquire the capacity to become more and more evil with the passing of time. This world would not be a place anyone would want to inhabit.

> And out of the ground the Lord God made every tree grow that is pleasant to the sight and good for food. The tree of life was also in the midst of the garden, and the tree of the knowledge of good and evil (Gen. 2:9).
>
> Then to Adam He said, "Because you have heeded the voice of your wife, and have eaten from the tree of which I commanded you, saying, 'You shall not eat of it': Cursed is the ground for your sake; in toil you shall eat of it all the days of your life" (Gen. 3:17).
>
> Then the Lord God said, "Behold, the man has become like one of us, to know good and evil. And now, lest he put out his hand and take also of the tree of life, and eat, and live forever . . ." (Gen. 3:22).
>
> So He drove out the man; and He placed cherubim at the east of the Garden of Eden, and a flaming sword, which turned every way, to guard the way to the tree of life (Gen. 3:24).

As frail, bendable humans, we are condemned to death as a result of disobedience and sin. But death isn't the end; it is just the beginning of life everlasting. It is the entry to a life so glorious we just cannot imagine the beauty that awaits us—that is, if we accept Christ as our Savior and call upon his name.

As it states in 1 Corinthians 15:55: "O Death, where is your sting? O Hades, where is your victory?"

CHAPTER 19

You Must Go Back

After I received the revelation about humankind and sin, an unseen force turned me around.

"You must go back," the presence said.

Stunned, I shouted, "No, please no. I have made it to heaven, and I don't want to go back." I couldn't believe it. This was beyond anything I could have ever imagined. I made it to heaven. I was standing right there, on heaven's territory! I was in, wasn't I? But I was being told I had to go back to earth. Back to that place of death, sickness, pain, poverty, and sin of every kind, back to that place where the Devil torments constantly. I couldn't fathom it. Why was I brought to this beautiful, spiritual place if I was not to remain? The questions went on and on, but I did realize one thing.

The reality was that we would have a free will in heaven. But on the other hand, just as it is here on earth, God's perfect will is the compass, and it will prevail.

Oh, how I wanted to stay there, in that perfect place, to walk the radiant city, to hear the prayers and songs of the saints, to see my Savior face-to-face! I wanted so much to stay. To go back to earth seemed pale, deathly, and so defeating. Would I ever be content in that environment again? How could I go back after experiencing the glory of heaven; how could I possibly go back? Peace surrounded me, enveloped me, and wrapped me in its loving arms. I was fine. The loved ones left behind would be fine, and we would see one another again. All would be right. If I never returned to earth, my family and friends would understand, and they would know that I was in heaven, feasting and praising with the saints.

Amazingly, I realized death is not difficult at all. No, life here on earth is a struggle and often disappointing and painful.

My mind asked the question, why do we fight so hard to hang onto this troubled world and the things in this world that are so meaningless? Why do we do it? Why, when there is this beautiful city, this wonderful home, a place made for us by Christ Jesus?

It was a strong question, or so I thought, but the Holy Spirit remained silent on this question. In that silence, a strong reply reverberated.

I did not want to return to earth, to my fragile body. I wanted to remain, enveloped in warmth, light, and love, in that city. Again, my mind voiced a desire to stay and feast with the saints and meet my Lord face-to-face.

Why do I have to go back? Why, Lord, why?

All of the begging did no good. The Holy Spirit was adamant. In spite of my entreaties to stay, I found myself drifting away from the city in reverse, still facing the light. As the city receded into the distant darkness, becoming only a light-filled speck, I felt my spirit return to earth and reunite with my body, still prone on the bed where I'd left it.

"Whereas you do not know what will happen tomorrow, for what is your life? It is even a vapor that appears for a little time and then vanishes away" (James 4:14).

The city was fading away from me, and as hard as I tried to burn the image into my memory, I could not. I tried to memorize the architecture, the colors, the windows and doors, the gates and walls, but I simply could not seem to focus on the details I wanted to commit to memory. Somehow, the vision proved elusive, much to my disappointment.

I was looking with all of my power, trying to see the gates to the city, but I was not near enough and the light was extremely bright. I simply could not make them out, but was told that one day I would see it all.

Chapter 20

You Must Tell Others

As the city fell away in the distance, the mandate stepped into my mind. Again, not a voice or a conscious thought, but as a declaration speaking in my thought. "You must share this glimpse of glory with as many as you can. You are to actively seek out ways to present this testimony to all who will hear it. This is your calling. This is your duty."

The Holy Spirit, my constant companion as I made my journey to the city, also told me, "Not all who hear will believe. Not all who hear will react in a positive manner, and you will find many who simply do not believe. Do not be afraid and do not feel daunted. Spread the message as far and wide as you are able to do. I am with you."

Reflecting on the Holy Spirit's words, I thought about how many people, confounded and confused by Satan, would be the most profound unbelievers and the most difficult to convince. Lovers of this world and the things this world can bring—power, money, and social class—might reject my experience and try to reason that I was an unfortunate soul who imagined something that never really happened. They might call me crazy. Maybe they would laugh and say, "Oh yeah, that guy, that guy who believes he died and went to heaven! Can you believe that guy?"

Realizing I could very well be up against the spirit of unbelief, I could not waver. I had been ordered by the Holy Spirit to get the word out, to tell of my experience in dying and being taken to heaven. I could not allow myself to be concerned with the unbelievers; I was to press on and continue to tell my story and the story the Holy Spirit gave me to tell. Those who did not believe would fall victim to Satan and his lies, and my spirit understood there was nothing I could do for them. My assignment from the Holy Spirit was to concentrate on those who could or would believe. I was to use every means possible to present what had happened to me during my brief time on the other side.

The name of this book is no coincidence. The Holy Spirit gave me the title, and although I had thought about changing it, *A Glimpse of Glory* remains. Who am I to go against the Holy Spirit and my heavenly Father? The Holy Spirit gave me a glimpse of glory. I will respect His wishes.

As I worked on this book, I found myself driven to complete it as quickly as possible and get the word out and into as many hands as possible. I was reminded of what I was told by the Holy Spirit, "Get the word out and use every means possible."

What I saw and heard about the prophecy of Adam and Eve in the garden of Eden simply blew me away. This information alone was earth-shattering and simply had to be told. Back on earth, in my present body, I have talked with many people, including our small group leader Ed Armstrong, who is an ordained pastor, and a former pastor of ours, Mike Ecklund. They all agree that they have never heard of this revelation.

I was also to give my testimony to all audiences who would invite me to speak. It might be television shows, radio programs, church groups both large and small, and individuals.

Once I returned to my physical body in the hospital, a now-calm Faith by my side, I could not stop telling everyone who would talk to me about the City of Heaven. I remember lying on the table in the cardio catheterization lab, waiting for an angiogram, babbling to the nursing staff and my cardiologist, describing the beauty of heaven. Did anyone really hear me? I don't know. Did they write me off as being medicated and not in control of what I was saying? Maybe. Still, I said it, and they heard it. Already, I was beginning to carry out my mandate from the Holy Spirit.

> How then shall they call on Him in whom they have not believed? And how shall they believe in Him of whom they have not heard? And how shall they hear without a preacher?
>
> And how shall they preach unless they are sent? As it is written: "How beautiful are the feet of those who preach the gospel of peace, who bring glad tidings of good things!" (Rom. 10:14-15).

CHAPTER 21

A Complete Absence of Evil

My spirit slipped back into my body without any fanfare, not a sound or a warning, just a sense of knowing that my soul once again was back in my physical body. During my quick return to earth and the rude realization that I had a vent tube shoved down my throat, I began to realize there was something so strikingly different about heaven. I could sense no evidence of the influence of evil. In fact, I sensed no knowledge of evil at all. Heaven appeared to be a complete vacuum, where evil could not exist. Because knowledge of evil does not exist in heaven, heaven holds perfect peace, ease, unfettered joy, and most of all, love. Heaven is what the garden of Eden was meant to be before the knowledge of evil came into the world.

The physical beauty of heaven simply cannot be described. I have never seen anything so unbelievably beautiful before or since. However, in heaven, although it seems that existence is moving at the speed of light, at the same time, heaven moves at its own pace, seemingly in slow motion. Additionally, Satan does not exist in heaven, and neither does the element of time. Nothing marks the passing of time in heaven, and therefore, freedom and peace abound. Satan cannot enter there; no longer can he tempt humankind to do something against God. He can no longer cause fear or torment. Heaven is the ideal end destination. The garden of Eden was meant to be the very same thing; however, once sin tainted the garden, God was forced to remove it or seal it and drive the humans away.

Once in heaven, there is no return ticket for the believer, sin being forgiven and forgotten by the Lord. When I think about heaven, I become euphoric because I know beyond a doubt that in heaven, the saints live completely free from all heartache and disappointment such as they may have experienced on earth. All a saint's tears will be wiped away, never to return. Unbelievable on earth, but pain, suffering, disease, sickness, death, sadness, and sin against God—in heaven, they are nonexistent. My brief time in heaven filled me with so much joy, more joy than I could possibly describe.

I learned here on earth that Satan comes against humankind with certain tools, such as fear, torment, and temptation. He uses these tools against the human race to drive a wedge between God and His creation. We were created to have a relationship with God.

Satan's overwhelming desire is that humankind blame God for his evildoing. In Satan's mind, if he can bring humankind to the point that humans are so disillusioned, angry, and worn out that they turn against God, Satan believes he will have won the ultimate victory. Satan is a liar. He craves the idea that humankind will come to believe God does not care, does not hear humankind's voices, and does not answer prayers. What Satan does not fathom is God's love is like the beautiful light that radiated from the city of New Jerusalem; it is filled with comfort, with eternal peace, and with joy everlasting. The element Satan is missing is that God will answer all who call. All humans must do is to reach out to God and seek His will.

If you have never experienced the voice of the Holy Spirit, just pray and ask the Holy Spirit to come into your heart, and then give yourself over to God completely, holding nothing back.

The glory of experiencing the closeness of my heavenly Father is the next best thing to actually being in heaven. I am often simply overcome with His love. God's word resonates with truth. His leadership makes me better because I trust Him and obey Him. When I take the reins and go out on my own without God's guidance, I fall on my face. When I act without God, I can make myself look very ignorant.

CHAPTER 22

Live a Life of Righteousness

"Blessed are those who do His commandments, that they may have the right to the tree of life, and may enter through the gates into the city" (Rev. 22:14).

During my brief time in heaven, I was given a mandate, an order, and that order was that I must warn all who would listen that God is truly a jealous God and we are to live a life of righteousness before Him. We should have no other gods before the one and only God, the God of Abraham, Isaac, and Jacob.

God wants us to confess our sin, ask forgiveness, and acknowledge Christ as our Lord and Savior. We must put our relationship with Christ first in our life and allow nothing to come between us.

I came back from heaven with a sense of urgency about the message, but I wondered how to get the message to the people. What would the appropriate vehicle be to shout the message from the mountaintops? The fact was, I wanted and needed to publish this book, and for that, I needed money to spread the message to the masses and carry out God's will, to complete the mandate He'd given me. It was imperative; the message had to be placed into as many hands as possible, in the most efficient way.

I knew I would not be able to reach the vast number of people God wanted this message to go to if I could only speak to them in person, and for that reason, I sold my most prized possession, my 1961 Corvette.

That car was a beauty, a car aficionado's dream. It had a fuel-injected 283 CI, 315 HP engine and everything that a car guy would want. I've loved cars all my life, but this one, it had my heart and soul.

So knowing what I had to do, I prayed and reasoned with God about getting the word out and what would be the best way to do that. God kept telling me to publish a book, to get the message into the hands of the masses by publication. I entreated God day and night about financing such a project. Where would the money come from? Every time I asked the question, the same answer came. God had it all worked out.

"You shall have no other gods before me" (Deut. 5:7).

I continued to interrogate God about financing this project. I searched my soul many times, and each time He came back with the same answer: "Sell your' 61 Corvette and you will have more than enough money."

It tore my soul to think of the hours spent on restoring the car to its present beauty, the money, the physical strength I gave to bringing that car to the pristine, perfect state it was in. I loved driving it. I loved touching its sleek, curvaceous body. I loved to sit behind the steering wheel and slip the gearshift into gear. I adored lifting the hood to see the sterling silver motor under the hood. Everything about that car brought me joy and satisfaction; yet I was to sell it? Part with a possession I prized, one that I adored?

Well, I knew it could be sold, and probably pretty easily, but it was still a struggle to let myself actually put it up for sale. The more important issue, though, was: would I follow God's will in this thing or not?

I have free will. I could have decided not to follow God's will, keep the car, and try to finance publishing this book another way. Or I could have sat on the whole thing and done nothing at all. Either way, I would still have my lovely '61 Chevy, and maybe someday, I would get around to doing God's will and getting this story out. But no, I was obedient to God's will. I knew my obedience in this matter would be a turning point between God and me.

I posted an ad for the car on one of the most popular auction websites. The auction ran for seven days. Within two days, the auction reached my reserve price, and on the final day it climbed much higher than I thought it ever would.

After all, earthly possessions are really without importance and can be a hindrance.

The car was sold. With tears in my eyes, I watched as the new owner loaded the '61 into his car hauler and pulled away, headed for Tennessee.

Now it was time to follow God's order and carry out the plan His Holy Spirit gave me while I was in heaven.

CHAPTER 23

Days of Recovery

After a long, uncomfortable seven days in the ICU, I was released and sent home on December 31. Faith and I were exhausted from the ordeal and slept much of the first two days at home.

In retrospect, it was as if I emerged from a tomb. I began to heal from the puncture wounds where blood had been drawn for all of the medical tests I had been subjected to in the hospital. I also had several locations where IVs had been placed, a vascular port in my shoulder, and a spinal tap puncture. I was amazed how fast I began to heal and how fast the bruising faded.

Then on January 8, the breathing problem returned. We called my doctor and were instructed to return to the Mercy Hospital emergency room immediately.

Once there, I was admitted directly into the ICU again, where more testing went on for several days. This time my doctor took nothing for granted and took no chances. He realized he was dealing with something potentially fatal.

Two new doctors were added to my care team, a pulmonary specialist and a cardiologist.

To date I have the results for 130 tests that were performed, all pointing to nothing indicating the cause of my respiratory illness.

I was placed back on steroids and antibiotics. I was taking such massive doses of steroids that I had to be placed on an insulin drip. My blood sugar was monitored every hour until it was regulated. I was asked several times a day if I were a smoker or whether I'd been diagnosed with COPD. Strange questions for me, as in my life, I have never smoked anything and have never been in an environment that could cause COPD.

The new cardiologist insisted on an angiogram procedure so any heart issues could be ruled out before I left the hospital. I was awake for this procedure and heard the comments made by the cardiologist: "He is slick; no problems here." I tried to tell them that I had a heart like a V8 engine, but they would not listen.

On January 15, I was finally released for the second time and, to date, have had no reoccurrence of any of the breathing problems. I will never again take for granted the ability to draw a deep, refreshing breath.

CHAPTER 24

Faith's Perspective
(written by my wife)

I was fifteen years old when Rusty, my adopted uncle, introduced me to Rick. He drove me across town to a gas station where Rick was working on an old 1958 MG that he bought from the owner of the station.

Rick was very tall and muscular, with blond hair and blue eyes. I remember describing him to a friend as being "big and gorgeous." After the day I was introduced to Rick, I knew there was no one else I could ever be interested in; I was immediately smitten. We dated for some time and were married August 8, 1969, when I was seventeen and he was nineteen.

The Vietnam War was the topic of the day in 1969. Young men were being drafted left and right, plucked out of their homes and lives and sent to go fight in the war. Rick and I were young, but we decided to marry because we were afraid he would be drafted as soon as he was eligible. As it turned out, we were right, because in September 1969, the dreaded draft papers arrived. Rick reported to the draft board as he was ordered to do, and after the testing, he was informed he would be classified as 1Y due to foot surgery he had as a child. For that reason, Rick was considered ineligible for military service.

Rick and I have lived a lot of life since that day in August 1969 when we took our eternal vow in front of God and our families, and it's been a wonderful ride. Now, at forty-three years of marriage, Rick is my best friend, constant companion, and soul mate. We've struggled through many storms, rejoiced in good times, leaned on each other in bad times, and loved God in all times. Our biggest blessing has been and is our family. Rick and I are blessed with a daughter and son, two grandchildren, and one great grandchild. Life has been good, and I thank God for Rick and our life together.

December 2012 brought a situation into our lives that was so enormous, so unbelievable, and simply so glorious that I still weep at the thought of it. We were busy getting ready for the holiday season: decorating, baking, wrapping gifts, and planning a wonderful family event with our children and grandchildren. We were to have our family celebration on December 25. I was looking forward to a festive, happy occasion.

After preparing for our family Christmas celebration on December 23, Rick and I decided to go for our usual walk. Two miles was our usual walk, and it wasn't hard for either of us. Normally, it was invigorating. However, after we'd gone one mile, Rick told me he needed to cut it short and return to the house. He said, "I'm feeling tired and weak."

We returned home and went on with our celebratory plans.

Later that evening, Rick was in a state. He could not lie down, sit, or stand erect, and he was complaining that he could not breathe. I finally packed Rick into the car and headed for the emergency room at Mercy Hospital.

The ER doctor ordered blood work, a chest X-ray, and several tests, along with a breathing treatment. The tests all indicated nothing out of the ordinary; however, the breathing treatment did give some relief and seemed to improve Rick's ability to breathe.

We were bewildered. The tests failed to reveal any pneumonia or any kind of infection, and therefore, the ER doctor released Rick with some antibiotics and an inhaler, stating that it must be just some form of "community-acquired pneumonia." We weren't even sure what community-acquired pneumonia was; however, we picked up the prescriptions at the pharmacy and returned home, only to quickly make a return trip to the emergency room at Mercy Hospital around twelve-thirty on Christmas Eve morning.

This time the ER notified Rick's internist, Dr. Froncek, of his condition. Dr. Froncek insisted Rick be admitted and ordered a host of other tests.

In the nightmare hours following, test after test was ordered and conducted as I watched, feeling completely helpless, praying, hoping, sobbing in turns. Rick was unable to stand erect, sit in a chair, or lie flat. Fear rose in my chest as I watched him struggle for breath. He'd come to the point he had to stand in a tripod position in order to breathe to remain conscious.

I couldn't believe what I was witnessing. Surely the doctors could do something to relieve his misery; surely there was a cure or a treatment or something that would put an end to this awful event. I wanted to scream, "This is your job, your vocation! Make him well!" I stood by, watching my husband gasp for air, knowing his heart rate was elevated and there was nothing I could do but hope and pray that the doctors would find a solution before he was too weak to fight the infection.

I heard him say, "I can't go on; I'm running out of strength." Looking at the monitors, I saw his heart rate was nearly double his normal resting rate; it had been that way for almost forty-eight hours. In forty-eight hours he had not been able to rest or sleep. I suddenly realized how fast Rick's condition was deteriorating. He was taking breathing treatment after breathing treatment. The duration of relief after a treatment was no more than forty-five minutes and was rapidly dropping. I feared soon the treatments would be of no use whatsoever.

Our son, Jason, was with me. In an instant, we realized how fast Rick's condition was failing. I left the room to call Tammy, our daughter, a registered nurse at Mercy. Frightened out of my mind, I babbled on, trying to explain his worsening condition and how frightened I was that he might be in extreme jeopardy. Much to my relief, Tammy told me she would be there in a matter of minutes.

When Tammy arrived, Rick was still in the tripod position over the bed gasping for breath. Tears rolled down my face; I couldn't control myself any longer. What I was witnessing was so horrific to me. I wanted to be strong for Rick, but I was out of strength and out of my mind.

Tammy took hold of my arms and said, "Get hold of yourself, Mother. Listen to me. Mother, calm down. Tell me what's been going on here." She took Rick's pulse and noticed his mouth held a bluish tint and his nail beds were turning blue. During this time, a technician came into the room to check his blood gases. Tammy immediately inquired as to the reading. The technician told her the blood oxygen level was 78. At that point, Rick began to collapse, and it took everyone in the room to get him on the bed.

As I watched the horrific scene in disbelief, I saw Tammy run from the room to the nurses' station. I couldn't take my eyes off Rick, but I heard Tammy snap, "I'm not trying to tell you how to do your job, but you better call the rapid-response team right now or I will do it myself! He should have been in the ICU hours ago."

Within minutes, medical personnel started streaming into the room and started working to stabilize Rick.

It was as if my mind were full of wind, rolling, reeling, and shrieking wind. I couldn't think straight. It was all too much: the glaring lights, the smells, the sounds of the hospital. What was happening here to him, to us? I was frantic; I could not imagine life without Rick. We were a couple of kids when we were married. Rick was my anchor, my foundation; we had faced life's biggest challenges together and some of life's greatest joys. How could I go on without him?

The rapid-response team arrived and informed us that all family members had to wait out in the hall while they worked. Gathering together and holding hands with my son and daughter-in-law in the hallway, we immediately started praying. We prayed and we prayed, asking God to keep Rick with us. My daughter was talking to the nurses at the nursing station.

We left the room at four o'clock on Christmas Day, and we were not allowed to see him again until nine-thirty that evening. After we left Rick's room, I asked Jessie, my daughter-in-law, to call relatives and friends and notify them of Rick's condition.

Friends and family began pouring into the waiting room soon after Jessie made her calls. I was astounded at the outpouring of love and support for Rick and me on Christmas Day, a day all of them would have probably preferred to spend with their own loved ones in front of a cozy fire, eating good food, unwrapping presents, and carrying out their own family traditions. Here we were on Christmas Day, and yet all of these people came and prayed with me for Rick. Church members came, friends came, and family came. They all prayed for Rick's recovery. The outpouring of love and support was so beautiful and warm, and for a moment I forgot my troubles, my concern for Rick. For a moment, I was buoyed on wings of steel, carried to a place where nothing could touch him or me—but just for a moment.

All afternoon long, people came and waited with me and prayed constantly for Rick's recovery.

Five and one half agonizing hours later, when he was stabilized in the ICU, I finally saw Rick again. I believe I wore a hole in the flooring during that time, pacing back and forth, sitting down, getting up, pacing some more, praying the entire time, unable to sit still, unable to stand still. When I finally saw Rick, I saw a ventilator tube in his mouth, tubes in his nose, and IVs running fluids into his arms; wires were attached everywhere, and a monitor was tracking his vital signs. The sight broke my heart.

Dr. Patel, his doctor while in the ICU, called me into a consultation room. There, among the taupe—and teal-inspired décor and the endless magazines about women's health, he informed me that Rick was gravely ill and there was the possibility that he could have suffered a stroke due to extremely high blood pressure. Dr. Patel went on to tell me that Rick's body was in septic shock, with a temperature approaching 104 degrees. Rick had experienced respiratory failure and had to be placed on a ventilator. I asked the doctor what his chances were for recovery, and he told me it would be several hours before he would know. *Several hours before he would know? An eternity.*

I slept, badly, on a couch in the waiting room, waiting and wondering all night what Dr. Patel might tell me come morning. Would Rick survive? Would he survive but be impaired? Would he require care if he survived this thing? What would be our next steps in any case?

After a hard night trying to get comfortable in the hospital waiting room, I arose to find Dr. Patel standing next to my chair. It was December 26, the day after Christmas.

"Good news, Mrs. East," Dr. Patel announced. "The brain scan indicates no stroke, and your husband's blood pressure went very high once, but it has now returned to low, normal actually.

Unfortunately, I do not know the source of the infection. That remains undetermined."

I watched Dr. Patel walk away in his white coat, heels clicking on the floor, and I wasn't certain that I understood one word he'd said to me. Rick was still sick, wasn't he? Why was there no solution?

In any event, I returned to Rick's room, held his hand, and turned my misgivings over to God. Thinking about all that happened, to this day I believe Tammy and Dr. Patel saved Rick's life.

At the time, I didn't know. I didn't understand what had happened to my husband, where he went, what actually took place with him. Nothing was clear for me.

Late in the afternoon when I went back to the ICU, Rick's nurse came to the waiting room and said that Rick had pulled the ventilator tube out of his throat and was coming around.

As I was allowed to go in, I approached his bed. He was having trouble seeing, and his voice was raspy from self-extracting the ventilator tube. Rick was still extremely pale. I wanted to gather him in my arms and hold him, and as I took his hand and leaned in to kiss him, he said, "Why didn't you just let me die?" I was astounded, crushed even. I didn't know what to say. My husband was nearly taken from me, I nearly lost him, and he now tells me he wished I'd let him die? My eyes welled with tears, but Rick seemed to know that I didn't understand why he wished he were dead.

Rick began to tell me his story in his rasping, gravely voice. From the instant of leaving his physical body to realizing he was in the spirit, drifting toward heaven and seeing how beautiful it is, how peaceful, how sin-free, and of being told he must return to earth, that he was not to stay but was to come back and tell his story, and how he begged to be allowed to stay but was told no, and the mandate to return to his physical body and tell all who would listen about his experience in heaven. The last thing he said about it was, "Heaven is so beautiful."

Amazement flooded through my body from head to toe. I knew what he said was true because Rick simply could not make this up. Understanding and love took over the place in my heart that was hurt by his insistence that he would rather be dead. I understood his reticence at coming back to us. I understood.

In the days that followed, the story began to flow like life-giving water. Rick witnessed to everyone who came close enough for him to talk to. He said the Holy Spirit told him to tell his story to everyone he could, and he has not been silent on this topic since.

Rick couldn't hold his story in. He told me when he went for his angiogram, he was lying on the examination table telling the doctor and nursing staff the whole story from start to finish. Funny thing, he was under anesthesia at the time. There was no telling what he said, but he was sure that the Holy Spirit was doing the talking.

I watched and I supported him, but I knew that Rick had mixed emotions for a long time about coming back from such a beautiful place. Nonetheless, his family and friends continue to rejoice that he returned to us.

Rick spent a week in the ICU and improved dramatically. He was then released and sent home. One week later the symptoms began to return, Frightened out of my mind again, I called my daughter. It was late in the evening again so she told me to call Dr. Froncek's office and to talk to the doctor on call, and let them know what was happening. I was told to get him to the ER immediately. Rick was admitted into the ICU again as he underwent another week of treatment.

Just after he arrived home this last time, one of his friends told him that no one had influenced his life in such a positive way as Rick had. That comment alone, from C. W. Craig, made his coming back worthwhile.

Chapter 25

A Scientific Mystery

The writing of this chapter was delayed until one final test was conducted on March 8, 2013. The result of that test failed to confirm the source of my illness as asthma.

I recall, during the second week of treatment in the ICU, my pulmonary specialist coming into my room and stating with a great deal of confidence that he had uncovered the cause of my health issues. "You have asthma," he stated, rocking back and forth on his heels.

Before I was tested, I read all I could about asthma, and it seemed to me that asthma was probably the correct diagnosis; I was certain the test would be positive and I would be given new medication to control my new condition, asthma. But one complication arose: the test came back completely negative.

After 130 different tests, my expansive medical team finally gave up hope that a viable reason for the illness that took my life will ever be found.

I am certain God took me to heaven, and once there, assigned me a mission and then sent me back to complete that mission.

My illness and recovery have been a miracle, one that modern medicine cannot explain.

Is it all a coincidence? I certainly do not think so. People looked at me just days after I was released from the ICU and said, "I can't tell you have ever been sick." My response was, "I wasn't just sick; I was dead and went to heaven."

What a way to start a conversation about the reality of heaven and hell. Sometimes their eyes would widen, sometimes they would take a step back, and sometimes they would mutter something unintelligible and walk away. It's a bit shocking for people to realize they have just had a conversation with a dead man, one who experienced heaven. Some would stay and talk with me, though, and that was part of my assignment from God, to tell the story. I was beginning to fulfill that mandate.

After I recovered partially and was feeling well enough to attend church for the first time since my hospitalization, I went forward after the altar call to thank my pastor for all of the prayers, flowers, and visits to the hospital. He wanted to hear about my near-death experience and my trip to heaven. He asked me to phone his secretary and set up an appointment so we could get together. I studied my schedule and made the call. I discovered that it would be two weeks before we both had an hour for a private conference.

Hosea is a very busy man, being the spiritual leader of a large church, and I am busy as well, I am retired, but at this time I was selling my Corvette, going to doctors appointments for follow-up visits and helping my wife care for our two grandsons, when needed. Our schedules did not match up and I wanted my wife to attend the meeting with me because she had a lot of information that I did not.

To protect his sanity and safeguard his personal time, Hosea has to watch his schedule closely as I have just described, because if he didn't, he would become an ineffective leader. It is just that simple. Not only Hosea, but any effective earthbound person in a leadership role must make time management a high priority.

When I think about our heavenly Father, I wonder how He manages to hear millions of prayers and then make decisions about those prayers and respond to those prayers within minutes or even seconds. I heard those people praying while I was in heaven; the sound of their prayers was earth-shattering and melodic at the same time.

Does God have a staff of angels, and does He delegate responsibility to those angels so all prayers can be heard and answered? In my earthly body and mind, I don't know, but I suppose someday that question will be answered. At any rate, our God is so incredible, so awesome, and so powerful. Earthly humans are just no match for His power.

An audience with God is just a whisper away, or I should say, just a thought away. When I think of that aspect of God, I am overcome with His incredible love and power.

CHAPTER 26

What a Victory

L iving here on earth, I realize some wonder about my sanity when I relay my experience in heaven and when I tell them that experience is the single greatest blessing of my life.

I am amazed and honored that God chose me to take to heaven on a guided tour of the Promised Land.

Just think of it: I saw the city of New Jerusalem in all of its glory, radiating with light from the throne of God. Faith is no longer required for me to believe; it is there, and I saw it and felt God's glorious love for us. What else can I say?

I always felt God had a mission in store for me, one that would allow me to serve Him and lift up the name of Jesus. I have often prayed for that calling and even begged for the opportunity, but I came to feel my prayers were going nowhere but to the ceiling. The longed-for mission didn't come to me, and after many years of prayer and supplication, I gave up hope that God would use me in any way. I wanted to serve; why wouldn't He use me? I again felt rejected—were my sacrifices and offerings rejected like those of Cain? Were they just second-rate and not my best?

> Now Adam knew Eve his wife, and she conceived and bore Cain, and said, "I have acquired a man from the LORD." Then she bore again, this time his brother Abel. Now Abel was a keeper of sheep, but Cain was a tiller of the ground. And in the process of time it came to pass that Cain brought an offering of the fruit of the ground to the LORD. Abel also brought of the firstborn of his flock and of their fat. And the LORD respected Abel and his offering, but He did not respect Cain and his offering. And Cain was very angry, and his countenance fell.
>
> So the LORD said to Cain, "Why are you angry? And why has your countenance fallen? If you do well, will you not be accepted? And if you do not do well, sin lies at the door. And its desire *is* for you, but you should rule over it" (Genesis 4:1-7).

There were times I thought I should take matters into my own hands and give something a try, but I knew how that endeavor would turn out. Whatever I might do wouldn't be what God wanted me to do, and therefore, it would be a pitiful attempt to gain favor in His eyes while being blinded to what He really wanted me to do. I'd given myself heart and soul over to God. I wanted to do His bidding, carry out His perfect will for me, and accomplish what He directed me to do. Over the years, doors remained closed and opportunities withered on the vine, and I had no mission from God, no mandate, no way to please Him.

My search ended and my prayers were answered upon my illness and trip to heaven. Now I have a mission, and the mission from God is clear.

Reality has a new meaning for me now, a new perspective. What is it like to die? Well, I know that now. What is it like to find yourself in heaven, and what is it like to come back to this world from heaven? I was there. I know it, I saw it, and I experienced it.

In spite of that, I find myself wondering what it is like to experience all heaven has to offer. I desperately wanted to see Jesus face to face when I was there, and I wonder, what is it truly like to stand in the presence of God? Could I have seen Moses and the prophets? Could I have talked with King David and walked with the disciples? Could I have seen my Lord face to face and heard him say, "Well done, my dear servant, well done"?

Reaching a little further, what about my family and my ancestors, people I never knew? Could I have met them, become acquainted with them?

I could go on and on. My imagination is running to random thoughts and wishes.

In my quiet moments, I still wonder about heaven and what it will be like to see and experience it all.

Faith senses my mind running amok from time to time. Seeing that faraway look in my eyes, she will ask, "What are you thinking about?" Faith knows what I am thinking about during those times, but she asks anyway. She asks because she knows I want to tell her, and I do tell her where my mind goes during those faraway moments.

In my life, there are negatives, and even in heaven when I was told to go back to my physical body on earth, I thought, *How am I going to pay all of those hospital bills?* I don't know where that thought came from. It slipped into my mind as I began my return to earth. How did I know my hospital bills would be through-the-roof expensive? My remark, humorous as it is, was also true.

CHAPTER 27

To Those Who Doubt

The debate will rage on and on as long as there are heaven and hell. Scientific studies will try to prove exactly when death actually occurs. An explanation will be sought after, and vast sums of wealth will be spent trying to explain away the sovereignty of God.

I have been asked, "Were you ever pronounced clinically dead?" I can only tell the truth and say, "No. My body was being kept alive by artificial means while my spirit was in heaven."

Some skeptics might say, "You were never actually dead, so how could you have seen heaven?" To that comment, I can only reply, "Well, someone forgot to tell God, because heaven is what I experienced and where the Holy Spirit told me I was and heaven is what I saw. You should debate that issue with God. By the way, good luck with that debate."

I can just hear that conversation now. "God, you should have never taken Rick's soul to heaven; he was never pronounced clinically dead." God would reply, "Do you know who you are talking to?"

There are videos on the Internet of people trying to discredit others like myself who have witnessed the glory of heaven. How sad. These people by their own admission are stating that they have no hope for an eternity in heaven, no hope for salvation or forgiveness, for peace and mercy and the grace of God, our heavenly Father.

Hell, by their own sad acknowledgment, is to become their final home for all of eternity. Lord God, I pray that they will bow before you before it is eternally too late for them.

The events related in the first few chapters of this book left my personality scarred and me with a disability. To disclose my past, even to my wife, was so painful I could not bear it. Many years went by, and finally when I was in my late thirties, the story slowly came out.

Public speaking was simply torture. When asked to speak publicly, I would decline. I knew that when I would begin to speak, I would become that little boy before the third-grade class. My mind would go blank with fear of being humiliated once again, and my fear would be realized. I could not do it.

Since my experience, I have been asked to speak many times before groups of varying sizes. I was told by the Holy Spirit to tell my story to all who would listen, so my greatest fear had to be faced.

A new sense of boldness has come about, my confidence has grown immeasurably, and I am overflowing with the reassurance provided by God's Spirit. Who can argue against His sovereignty, His authority, and prevail?

As I wrote this book, old painful memories had to be revisited. Memories that had been suppressed and tucked away where they could harm me no more had to be pulled out of storage and dusted off. Often I found myself working at my computer as the tears flowed down, but I remembered the glory of heaven and it was worth every tear, every moment of pain. I would not miss it for any amount of misery. This mission must be carried out!

CHAPTER 28

An Urgent Mission

Being a deacon at Ridgecrest Baptist Church, I receive information almost every day about the passing of a member or the loved one of a member, and I am reminded that we live in a world of constant change. God created a self-sustaining world. One day we hear of one's passing, and the next we see a new child born.

Faith and I were young only yesterday. We were eager to face our life together. Today we are great grandparents. How quickly earth time passes; we have only a short time to learn the lessons of life.

> To everything there is a season,
> A time for every purpose under heaven:
> A time to be born,
> And a time to die;
> A time to plant,
> And a time to pluck what is planted;
> A time to kill,

And a time to heal;
A time to break down,
And a time to build up;
A time to weep,
And a time to laugh;
A time to mourn,
And a time to dance;
A time to embrace,
And a time to refrain from embracing (Ecclesiastes 3:1-4).

Every day lost men, women, and children are passing from this earthly life without hope and eternal security. The mission given to me in heaven is urgent.

As soon as I had the strength, I began telling my story to anyone who would listen. One evening Faith sent me to a nearby store for milk. I picked up the milk and was leaving when I heard someone call my name; it was some friends from church who had heard about my illness. They did not know of my near-death experience. I began to tell them the whole story.

They were sitting in a booth eating ice cream. As I talked, they stopped eating and sat there with amazed looks on their faces. In a nearby booth sat three women; they heard what I was saying and began listening. One of the ladies received a cell phone call, and I heard her say, "I have got to call you back; you won't believe what this guy is saying."

I finished my story and noticed other people had gathered. Some had tears streaming down their faces, and some were looking on with mouths wide-open.

The three women, I surmised, were a mother and her two daughters. The oldest daughter asked me if I were a minister.

"No," I replied. Then she began to tell me that her mother had breast cancer and the prognosis was not good. She asked me to pray for her. I complied with her request, praying for her right there in the store. When I finished praying, I looked around and felt that a revival was about to break out. Those who were looking on quickly scurried away, but were deeply moved by what they had just seen and heard. I could feel the Spirit and see tears in their eyes but when I finished praying, instead of yielding to the Spirit, the bystanders scurried away, going about their business.

I never saw the three women again, but pray for them often.

I have told my story many times since and have repeatedly received the same request. Almost every time when I have finished, someone comes to me with tears streaming down and says, "Your story was for me; it has changed my life. I want to live that better life."

That is why it is so urgent that this story gets out to those hurting people.

CHAPTER 29

God's Grace

O nce out of the hospital, I began to read many stories that were similar to mine. A realization hit me one day as I read another story of near-death experience. My experience was unique; all of the others had experienced horrific accidents or extreme illness, all requiring long recovery periods—weeks, months, even years of recovery. Some had many surgeries and would never be completely healed again. I came out of the hospital and was almost back to normal within days.

Another unique aspect of my illness came to light as Faith and I told my story to some friends. Throughout the entire experience, I had no fear. I knew I was going to die if something did not correct my breathing problems, but there was no fear. Death did not frighten me. God had told me that I was His and all fear was gone. Throughout the whole experience, even when I realized that I had passed and was in heaven, there was no fear. I still remain amazed how easily I slipped away from earth to heaven and back again.

I am just a simple man; I am not a doctor or a minister; I would not even be considered an educated person. I am like Moses, I am someone that others would look upon and say, "Why this guy? He is totally not qualified for this." All of those critics would be completely correct, but God had other plans and I will be obedient.

CHAPTER 30

Obedience

While this book was being written, Faith and I were asked to care for our great grandson, Easton. We were asked to keep him overnight for several nights while our granddaughter moved. The first night, Easton began to cough when we laid him down to sleep. He coughed and coughed and coughed. When our children hurt, Faith and I hurt along with them. We love them and can't bear to see them suffer. He did not have a fever or any other symptoms; we gave him the only medication you can give a seventeen-month-old toddler, Ibuprofen for Toddlers.

It did nothing. I put my hand on his tiny little body and began to pray for him, and that did no good either. He was so tired that he slept even though he was still coughing.

The next night was the same, so I began praying again, only this time I called upon Jesus to have mercy on my little grandson. I said, "This little child is so innocent, and Satan has caused him to have an illness that makes him cough uncontrollably. I know your will is that he should be healed."

Faith sat in a rocking chair holding the child and tried her best to comfort him as he coughed. Suddenly the answer came: "Give the child a drink of Coke." I have learned not to question God, simply to obey, so obey I did. We had some bottles of Coke in the refrigerator. I immediately poured some into a glass and put a straw in so Easton could drink. He drank several ounces, and his coughing immediately stopped. The next evening we repeated the process, and his coughing never returned.

Was there healing power in that bottle of Coke? I think not. Was this just another coincidental outcome? No one will ever convince me of that. It was an act of faith and an answered prayer. Jesus healed the little guy, not the Coke.

> Now Naaman, commander of the army of the king of Syria, was a great and honorable man in the eyes of his master, because by him the Lord had given victory to Syria. He was also a mighty man of valor, but a leper. And the Syrians had gone out on raids, and had brought back captive a young girl from the land of Israel. She waited on Naaman's wife. Then she said to her mistress, "If only my master were with the prophet who is in Samaria! For he would heal him of his leprosy." And Naaman went in and told his master, saying, "Thus and thus said the girl who is from the land of Israel."
>
> Then the king of Syria said, "Go now, and I will send a letter to the king of Israel."
>
> So he departed and took with him ten talents of silver, six thousand shekels of gold, and ten changes of clothing. Then he brought the letter to the king of Israel, which said,
>
> Now be advised, when this letter comes to you, that I have sent Naaman my servant to you, that you may heal him of his leprosy.

And it happened, when the king of Israel read the letter, that he tore his clothes and said, "Am I God, to kill and make alive, that this man sends a man to me to heal him of his leprosy? Therefore please consider, and see how he seeks a quarrel with me."

So it was, when Elisha the man of God heard that the king of Israel had torn his clothes that he sent to the king saying, "Why have you torn your clothes? Please let him come to me, and he shall know that there is a prophet in Israel."

Then Naaman went with his horses and chariot, and he stood at the door of Elisha's house. And Elisha sent a messenger to him, saying, "Go and wash in the Jordan seven times, and your flesh shall be restored to you, and you shall be clean." But Naaman became furious, and went away and said, "Indeed, I said to myself, 'He will surely come out to me, and stand and call on the name of the Lord his God, and wave his hand over the place, and heal the leprosy.' Are not the Abanah and the Pharpar, the rivers of Damascus, better than all the waters of Israel? Could I not wash in them and be clean?" So he turned and went away in a rage. And his servants came near and spoke to him, and said, "My father, if the prophet had told you to do something great, would you not have done it? How much more then, when he says to you, 'Wash, and be clean'?" So he went down and dipped seven times in the Jordan, according to the saying of the man of God; and his flesh was restored like the flesh of a little child, and he was clean (2 Kings 5:1-14).

Just like the Coke, the water of the Jordan River did not heal Naaman; it was his act of faith and his obedience to God that healed him of his leprosy.

CHAPTER 31

Only Trust Him

When I was saved in 1967, I put the control of my life completely into the hands of my Lord and Savior, Jesus Christ, and I was changed. My heart was changed, and I changed from the inside out. I received forgiveness, and only then I was able to forgive.

In the Old Testament, the Jewish nation tried to live under the written Law of Moses and failed. The written Law of Moses appealed to the intellect of humans. God had to change all of that so humanity could be changed and be forgiven, so He sent Jesus to change the *hearts* of humans, not their minds.

My father died on December 20, 1987, and I wept for most of the day, not for the usual reasons, but because of his inability to love his family and to be a father.

Every Christmas holiday, he would find something to become angry about and spoil the celebration for everyone. Even his death came during the Christmas holiday. I remember telling Faith this would be the last Christmas he would spoil. He completely missed the best aspects of life. I talked to him many times, trying to reason with him and change his mind about his life, but I always failed. I had also prayed for him to receive Christ as his savior, and he just could not trust in Him. For these reasons, I wept for him, and then it was over.

I forgave my father long before his death. I had been shown that there was something wrong, something wrong with him, not me.

Today I hear many people say, "Serve the God of your choice," or "Find your own way to heaven; there are many ways, you can just be a good person." Satan loves to hear these lies repeated and confessed by those whom he has deceived.

It says in John 14:6, "Jesus said to him, 'I am the way, the truth, and the life. No one comes to the Father except through Me.'"

God has given me an unbelievable opportunity and honor. I too have been raised from the dead like Christ. Don't get me wrong; being raised from death is only one similarity, and I can't begin to be compared to Jesus. My resurrection is more like that of Lazarus.

"Then Jesus said to them plainly, 'Lazarus is dead'" (John 11:14).

"Now when He had said these things, He cried with a loud voice, 'Lazarus, come forth!'" (John 11:43).

"Then, six days before the Passover, Jesus came to Bethany, where Lazarus was who had been dead, whom He had raised from the dead" (John 12:1).

Like Lazarus, I was raised from the dead by Jesus and given a specific purpose, a mission and an anointing to fulfill that mission.

There is one strange aspect of this experience I have encountered only in the church community. Often I perceive doubt and unbelief in the spirit of other Christians, and I am troubled by this. Do they really not believe in the power and miracles of our God? Or do they simply doubt my story?

I have prayed for the healing of fellow Christians. When asked to pray, I would discover great compassion for them as I was praying. When I began to pray, the Holy Spirit would come over me, and I would weep in the Spirit as I prayed. After the prayer, I could not remember all of the words I had just prayed, only the essence of the prayer. The people I prayed for would continue going to see their doctors, and the doctor would say their condition was not curable. Then somehow they would receive healing. Do they realize the source of their healing? The nonbeliever will give glory to the doctor. The true believer will give God the glory and know God as the source of all healing.

Years of communication with God have taught me that He knows me better than I know myself, and when He calls to me, I know His voice. He has proven this to me over and over and over. My advice is "Only trust Him." Trust in God alone. If you don't trust in me, it is already forgiven, but to not trust in God is an eternal mistake.

"But seek first the kingdom of God and His righteousness, and all these things shall be added to you" (Matt. 6:33).

CHAPTER 32

Heaven Can Be Yours

Thousands will be granted salvation today. You too can be assured that when the time comes, you will see heaven's glory. The steps are easy; just follow the Roman Road.

"For all have sinned and fall short of the glory of God" (Rom. 3:23a).

"But the gift of God is eternal life through Jesus Christ our Lord" (Rom. 6:23b).

"God demonstrates His own love for us, in that while we were yet sinners Christ died for us!" (Rom. 5:8).

"Whoever will call on the name of the Lord will be saved!" (Rom. 10:13).

"If you confess with your mouth Jesus as Lord, and believe in your heart that God raised Jesus from the dead, you shall be saved; for with the heart man believes, resulting in righteousness, and with the mouth he confesses, resulting in salvation" (Rom. 10:9-10).

If you know that God is knocking on your heart's door, ask Him to come into your heart.

Call out to God in the name of Jesus! Simply pray in His name, and confess that you are a sinner.

Ask God to forgive you and save you. Give your life to God. His love poured out in Jesus on the cross is your only hope to have forgiveness and change. His love bought you out of being a slave to sin. His love is what saves you. God loves you!

Congratulations you are now saved.

You now need to look for a local church where God's word is preached. The Bible says that we are to desire God's word like a newborn baby desires mother's milk.

When you find a church, you need to tell them that you have accepted Christ Jesus as your personal savior and that you need to be baptized.

I would like to know about your decision. Please e-mail me at r_east@swbell.net.

I would love to rejoice with you in your decision and pray for you.

Here we are at Fort Morgan, Alabama in June
2013 shortly after my recovery.

From left to right Mark Hunter, Hayley Hunter, Tammy Hunter, Faith
(holding Easton Hunter), Rick, Trey Hunter, Jessie and Jason East.

Mark's son (by a previous marriage) Corey and his new bride Jodi.

Rick and Faith July 2013.

Rick, on the right, and his cousin Keith Day at Starvey Creek
Bluegrass Festival July 2012. Rick and Keith's uncle Don Day and
their aunt Bobbie Day hold the festival two times a year at the
family farm near Conway, Missouri. Rick stayed with Keith and his
family while his mother recuperated and the two became close.

Faith behind the wheel of the 1961 Corvette. It was sold to publish this book. "Thou shall have no other Gods before me."

EPILOGUE

An epilogue is a glimpse into the future, something that happens after the story is over. It is a writing that pulls together or concludes events that happened earlier in the book or in the story and brings those events to their conclusion.

Almost all of the events recorded in this book were written down very close to the time they actually happened. I didn't know why at the time I was writing, but I knew it was important to record the actual events before time passed and things would be forgotten. I was driven to write, to record my experiences. Knowing these events were significant, they were recorded, written down to be used in the future. Not knowing the purpose for recording them, I was still driven to write to record before my recollection would fade and they would be lost forever.

How does this apply to the future? I will end the book with one story that I failed to write down when it happened. It is an event that takes place in the future. I don't recall when this vision actually occurred because I did not write it down. My only recollection is that it took place four or five years ago.

I was praying, as I often do, very early one morning. Usually around three o'clock in the morning, I will begin to wake up, and this is when I do my best praying. All is quiet, and there are no distractions. I pray with an open heart and an open mind and am overcome with the beautiful spirit of God. Knowing who I was and who I am now simply fills me with gratitude. Giving God the glory and honor and praise often evolves into weeping in the spirit and communications through the Holy Spirit. This was one of those occasions.

I had a vision of the great white throne of judgment. Christ was seated on his throne in heaven, and a multitude, more than could be counted, were gathered around. One person at a time from the multitude would be brought forward and asked this one simple question: "Who do you say that I am?" They did not need to reply; their lives were played out before them and before the multitude. With all humanity looking on, their sin was revealed and their lives weighed in the balance scales of judgment. When their life story was finished, great books were opened, and their names were not found. There was no need for comment; their lives revealed just how important their relationship with Christ really was. Then they would be taken away and cast into the lake of fire for all eternity.

> Then I saw a great white throne and him who was seated on it. The earth and the heavens fled from his presence, and there was no place for them. And I saw the dead, great and small, standing before the throne, and books were opened. Another book was opened, which is the book of life. The dead were judged according to what they had done as recorded in the books. The sea gave up the dead that were in it, and death and Hades gave up the dead that were in

them, and each person was judged according to what they had done. Then death and Hades were thrown into the lake of fire. The lake of fire is the second death. Anyone whose name was not found written in the book of life was thrown into the lake of fire (Rev. 20:11-15).

This passage from Revelation was not familiar to me at the time of my vision, and the question asked of the multitude, "Who do you say that I am?" was not familiar either. It was a few days later that I discovered the origin of that question. It opened my eyes and made me realize that my vision was authentic.

"He said to them, 'But who do you say that I am?' Peter answered and said to Him, 'You are the Christ'" (Mark 8:29).

A fitting epilogue, an event in the future, the final judgment for all who don't believe, the second death, and the lake of fire for all eternity. Is this the end of your story?

For now my story continues, and perhaps sometime in the future, I will add more to this book. Only God knows what the future holds. May God always bless and keep you in the palm of His hand!

God's perfect knowledge of humans is summed up in Psalm 139:

O Lord, You have searched me and known me.
You know my sitting down and my rising up;
You understand my thought afar off.
You comprehend my path and my lying down,
And are acquainted with all my ways.
For there is not a word on my tongue,
But behold, O Lord, You know it altogether.
You have hedged me behind and before,
And laid Your hand upon me.

Such knowledge is too wonderful for me;
It is high, I cannot attain it.
Where can I go from Your Spirit?
Or where can I flee from Your presence?
If I ascend into heaven, You are there;
If I make my bed in hell, behold, You are there.
If I take the wings of the morning,
And dwell in the uttermost parts of the sea,
Even there Your hand shall lead me,
And Your right hand shall hold me.
If I say, "Surely the darkness shall fall on me,"
Even the night shall be light about me;
Indeed, the darkness shall not hide from You,
But the night shines as the day;
The darkness and the light are both alike to You.
For You formed my inward parts;
You covered me in my mother's womb.
I will praise You, for I am fearfully and wonderfully made;
Marvelous are Your works,
And that my soul knows very well.
My frame was not hidden from You,
When I was made in secret,
And skillfully wrought in the lowest parts of the earth.
Your eyes saw my substance, being yet unformed.
And in Your book they all were written,
The days fashioned for me,
When as yet there were none of them.
How precious also are Your thoughts to me, O God!
How great is the sum of them!
If I should count them, they would be more in number
than the sand;
When I awake, I am still with You.

Oh, that You would slay the wicked, O God!
Depart from me, therefore, you bloodthirsty men.
For they speak against You wickedly;
Your enemies take Your name in vain.
Do I not hate them, O Lord, who hate You?
And do I not loathe those who rise up against You?
I hate them with perfect hatred;
I count them my enemies.
Search me, O God, and know my heart;
Try me, and know my anxieties;
And see if there is any wicked way in me,
And lead me in the way everlasting (Ps. 139:1-24).

About the Author

Rick East was born in March 1950 in Springfield, Missouri. He was born into a dysfunctional and abusive family environment. Physical disabilities and educational disappointments plagued him throughout his early years. He suffered a devastating blow to his already-battered ego when he was involved in a fatality auto accident in 1967. God kept him from completing a suicide attempt.

A Baptist Bible College student saw Rick's misery and led him to salvation and knowledge of Jesus Christ. This salvation changed his heart and turned his life around. If you ask him, he will tell you that he is just your average guy. "I don't know why God has chosen to communicate with me the way He has. I suppose it is just because I have asked Him to so many times and have had a heartfelt desire to communicate with Him."

On Christmas Day, 2012, Rick suffered respiratory failure and found himself in heaven communicating one-on-one with the Holy Spirit. Rick saw the holy city of heaven, New Jerusalem, and was told many things. Rick was instructed to write this book and be a witness to as many people as possible. The rapid-response team at Mercy Hospital in Springfield, Missouri, revived him and brought him back to this world. Rick did not want to return. The source of his illness has never been determined after 130 tests returned negative results.

Within days after discharge from the hospital, he was completely recovered.

Today Rick is retired from the steel industry, where he has worn many hats. He has served as a design draftsman, mechanical design engineer, structural steel detailer, sales estimator, assistant division manager, division manager, manager of projects and sales, managing partner, and business owner. He has successfully completed projects all over Southwest Missouri and the world. Rick will be the first to admit that his success was purely attributable to "the grace of God."

Rick and his wife, Faith, will be married forty-four years in August 2013. They have two children, two grandchildren, and one great grandchild.

Rick says, "My testimony proves that even the average person can make it to heaven if you only believe."

Aside from being a car guy, Rick is an avid sportsman and enjoys hunting and fishing, especially offshore and fly-fishing.

About the Coauthor

———⟫•⟪———

Yvonne S. Erwin is a women's fiction writer, living in Springfield, Missouri, with her two sons and her beloved lab, Ella. Yvonne began writing stories and poems at ten years old and continued writing into her adult years. She currently works as a legal assistant at a law firm in Springfield.

In 2009, she collaborated with her friend and mentor Wanda Sue Parrott and friend Amanda Barke on "The Trail of Tears" project, publishing an article on the disappearance of Native American traditions. Yvonne was the 2006 runner-up in *Glimmer Train* magazine's Summer Fiction Open and also won second place in the fiction category of the 2012 Springfield Writers' Guild Annual Poetry & Prose Contest. She currently serves as president of Springfield Writers' Guild, a chapter of the Missouri Writers' Guild, and is a member of Ozarks Romance Authors. She can be found on Facebook, and on her blog: www.y-write.blogspot.com.

Synopsis for A Glimpse of Glory

———⇒►●◄⇐———

Sixty-two-year-old Rick East is stricken with a mysterious illness. Rick is a lifelong Christian. He seeks medical attention at Mercy Hospital in Springfield, Missouri, where his condition rapidly deteriorates. Before doctors can identify the illness, he goes into respiratory arrest, passes from this life, and finds himself in heaven.

Was this illness allowed to happen so Rick could warn others to turn from sin, embrace Christianity, and serve God? Rick has always thought that God had a calling or mission for him to carry out, but until now did not know what it was.

The Holy Spirit gave the whole story in *A Glimpse of Glory*. The Holy Spirit even gave the title of this book to Rick.

CPSIA information can be obtained at www.ICGtesting.com
Printed in the USA
LVOW08s1348300813

350017LV00001B/1/P